Mathematics in the Making

Mathematics in the Making

Authoring Ideas in Primary Classrooms

Heidi Mills, Timothy O'Keefe,
and David J. Whitin

HEINEMANN   Portsmouth, NH

HEINEMANN
A division of Reed Elsevier Inc.
361 Hanover Street
Portsmouth, NH 03801-3912
Offices and agents throughout the world

We are grateful to the publishers and individuals below for granting permission to reprint material from previously published works.

"Growing Up" from *Younger Beginner Prep Course* by Willard A. Palmer, Morty Manus, and Amanda Vick Lethco. Copyright © 1973 by Alfred Publishing Co., Inc. Used with Permission of the Publisher.

Figure E-5, Copyright 1994, USA TODAY. Reprinted with permission.

Cataloging-in-Publication Data is on file with the Library of Congress
ISBN: 0-435-07100-9

Acquisitions Editor: Leigh Peake
Production Editor: Renée M. Nicholls
Cover Designer: Darci Mehall
Manufacturing Coordinator: Louise Richardson

Printed in the United States of America on acid-free paper
03 02 01 00   EB   2 3 4 5 6

Contents

Foreword

Early in my teaching career, each year on the day before school started, the curriculum specialist would come to my classroom laden with books and announce, "Well, here they are." "They" were my math workbooks, and I was happy to write each child's name on a shiny, colorful cover. After all, the entire math curriculum was housed within those pages!

I started out "teaching" from those workbooks in a sequential fashion, attempting to follow the teacher's edition. We covered about two pages a day. I had to hand in carbon copies of my plan book each week, and writing consecutive page numbers with a note "see TE, page _____," was easy. However, while the planning may have been simple, the teaching was difficult. For some students the work was too easy; for othes, too hard; and their correct answers didn't assure me that the children understood the concepts. The workbooks, which limited students to one correct answer, provided few opportunities for the children to explore mathematical ideas or to think creatively, and there were no ways for them to construct their own understandings or to explain their thought processes. As it became clear to me that the entire curriculum wasn't housed in workbooks, I began to bring in math manipulatives, and I started skipping some of the workbook pages.

Over the years, math has changed a lot in my classroom. As I've developed a holistic approach to reading and writing, I've incorporated the same underlying principles to the teaching and learning of math. I am therefore thrilled to have *Mathematics in the Making* in my hands, and along with many other elementary teachers, I will be referring to it regularly to help guide mathematics in my classroom.

In *Mathematics in the Making*, teachers now have a book that explicitly discusses the parallel development in the fields of reading, writing, and mathematics—one that provides a clear theoretical framework we can apply to the teaching and learning of mathematics. The book describes authentic experiences and conversations among children and teachers, and it offers projects and activities that teachers can easily adapt to their own classroom settings and district curriculum.

For years, teachers have been using the metaphor of authorship to describe children reading and writing in their classrooms. *Mathematics in the Making* breaks new ground by extending this metaphor to mathematics, "because it conveys the active, constructive, exploratory role that children must assume if they are to be the empowered mathematical thinkers that we know they can be."

Mathematics in the Making welcomes us into Tim O'Keefe's classroom over a three-year period as he teaches children in a transitional first, second, and third grade. Throughout the book, the authors, Heidi Mills, Tim O'Keefe, and David Whitin, along with the children, show us just how much math is "there." As one of the children eloquently says: "There are different kinds of math. There's the math like 2 + 2. That's the kind of stuff you find in books. But there's math all over. *Even though you can't see it, it's still there. You can just feel it. There's math there."*

The authors invite us to "Enjoy the day!" as we focus on mathematics in Tim's second grade, and we can't help but enjoy this classroom as the children sing; take the lunch count and share the lunch menu; discuss the calendar; share a variety of surveys; and plan ways to celebrate the fairy tales they have written. We also learn how these authors use literature as a starting point for a class project about non-standard measurement and how they integrate that project with a homework assignment. We learn *what* the children are learning—proportion and ratio, place value, odd and even numbers, equivalence, temperature, time and inequality, weight, and length. We also learn about the value of conversation, the benefits of children learning from each other, and the essential role of the teacher.

In this book, we also meet Aaron. He might not score well on timed tests, but the many surveys he conducts throughout the year demonstrate that his "real strength [lies] in his ability to think about situations and events mathematically." Through his conversations with classmates and the written word problems that he creates from his surveys, he shows us that he is a teacher and an author of mathematical ideas. We learn that the children's uniqueness can be celebrated and nurtured, while at the same time they can learn mathematical skills, strategies, and concepts required by the district curriculum.

In the chapter "Exploring Concepts over Time: Infinity Strikes Again," we read some of the children's conversations that develop from ongoing interests, and Heidi, Tim, and David show us the fundamental role that teachers play in these discussions. We see how working with a topic over time increases the children's understanding, generates deep personal interest, encourages children to build in each other's ideas, and allows mathematical theoreticians and authors to emerge. We also see the various opportunities available to integrate reading, writing, art, music, science, and social studies with mathematics. As Jonathan explained one day, "Look, Mr. O'Keefe! There's this picture of a mummy reading a book. The book that he's reading has a picture of the same mummy reading the same book. So it looks like infinity strikes again!"

As we move toward the twenty-first century, math curriculum is no longer found within the pages of colorful workbooks that concentrate primarily on computational skills. It is now derived from many sources, including interests and understandings of the children, professional knowledge of the teachers, and the district-wide curriculum. The children in Tim's class are learning "math like 2 + 2," but they are learning much more. Tim is teaching the district curriculum, but he is teaching much more. With teachers like Heidi, Tim, and David, the children are becoming mathematical authors as they discover that "there's math all over."

—Bobbi Fisher

Preface

This book is the story of how one elementary teacher, Timothy O'Keefe, and two university professors, Heidi Mills and David Whitin, worked together over a three-year period to build responsive classroom environments that valued children as sense makers, problem solvers and thoughtful decision makers. Their collaboration began in a transition first-grade classroom. In this context, children who were identified by their kindergarten teachers and a standardized test as not being ready for first grade were placed together in a transition first-grade room to receive additional support and time if necessary. It is important to note that we do not agree with this grouping practice. However, it was powerful to view firsthand the power and potential of holistic instruction with young children who had already been labeled as "at risk" learners.

We told our initial stories about the transition first-grade children in *Living and Learning Mathematics: Stories and Strategies for Supporting Mathematical Literacy* (Whitin, Mills, and O'Keefe 1990). However, although we have devoted several chapters here to the transition first-grade classroom, there are important distinctions between our last and current book. First, after working in the transition first-grade classroom, Tim moved to a new district where he taught heterogeneous groups of second and third graders. His collaborators followed. Therefore, this book has a broader scope; it portrays mathematics instruction in Tim's transition first- through standard second- and third-grade classrooms. We believe that the fact that this book includes three grade levels is a strength. It gives readers a broader view of mathematical literacy than we provided in our first book, showing what this model looks like across grade levels and highlighting the fact that the philosophy is the same regardless of grade level.

This book is theoretical yet *very practical*. Tim has written a chapter that provides the "behind the scenes" perspective of the classroom teacher. He responds to questions such as: How does Tim get started in the fall? How does he introduce students to the creation of surveys? How does he keep daily routines such as the "number of days" from getting stale? How does he help the child who struggles with mathematical concepts?

While many of the lessons that we learned in *Living and Learning Mathematics* still hold true for us, we have extended our thinking by adopting the metaphor of authorship in mathematics. In our first book, we adapted Halliday's work in language to discuss what was transpiring in the classroom. Although it was a very useful framework at the time, we became dissatisfied with this overall model because it did not effectively capture the many dimensions of the learning process that we wanted to convey; that is, the role of revision, the importance of prolonged learning engagements, and the generation of new ideas in a collaborative community. These ideas were certainly embedded in *Living and Learning Mathematics*, but they did not seem to be highlighted for readers to view them in a more global, yet practical way.

Since that time, we also realized more and more that mathematics is a way of thinking; Carolyn Burke helped us to see the importance of concepts as the bedrock of what it means to think mathematically. As we began to look for and identify these concepts, we realized that we needed to make the distinction among skills, strategies, and concepts very explicit. We wanted a model that would stress their uniquenesses as well as the interrelationships. We explored these ideas further when we wrote and implemented two Eisenhower Grants. We used Lynn Arthur Steen's *On the Shoulders of Giants* (1990), which stressed the crucial role of fundamental ideas in mathematics such as number, symmetry, ratio, function, and infinity. Our Eisenhower Grant teachers helped us see more clearly the importance of conceptual thinking.

Again, we found that our understanding of reading and writing helped us rethink and reframe our work in mathematics. The metaphor of authorship more effectively captured the social nature of learning as well as the personal invention of mathematical ideas that are the result of living in a supportive learning community. It was also more inviting and understandable.

Another important book that influenced our thinking was Vera John-Steiner's (1985) *Notebooks of the Mind*. By detailing the ways in which mathematicians come to know and perceive the world from a unique vantage point, it demonstrated that mathematics is a way of thinking; mathematicians view the world with the conceptual lenses of mathematics.

One other book that stretched our thinking was *Innumeracy* by John Paulos (1988). He outlines the characteristics of what he terms "innumerate" people. We found that numerate people have a good conceptual understanding of mathematical ideas; they are sense makers who have a good feel for the reasonableness of answers and a healthy skepticism about anything numerical. The combination of these resources, our work in elementary classrooms, and our involvement with the Eisenhower Grant teachers helped shape our thinking for this present endeavor.

In Chapters 2 and 4, we have identified the burning questions that teachers often ask after reading *Living and Learning Mathematics*: But how does it all fit together? What does a typical day look like? How do I weave mathematics into the fabric of my classroom life? In response to these questions, we created portraits of typical days in two different classrooms.

At first glance, it might appear as if there is a great deal of overlap here with classroom activities in our first book. Although there are surface-level similarities between the two books, the second book adds new depth to the topics introduced previously. For instance, there are a number of surveys that appear in both books. We still believe that surveys are valuable. However, there is a shift in the way these surveys are interpreted. In *Mathematics in the Making*, there are three new emphases: revision, using the language of mathematics, and creating and examining data over time. Since we are using the authoring metaphor, we began to look more closely at how learners displayed and revised the data they had collected. As Eisner tells us, we were learning that the form of the work informs us; that is, the way that the data is represented influences what we can say about it. As authors of mathematical texts, we have also come to realize that the language we use is an important feature of our endeavors. We place a third new emphasis in our current book—a discussion of the importance of collecting data over time.

In our first book, we shared a variety of children's mathematical stories. Most of the time, they were created in response to one of our formal instructional invitations. In our present book, we highlighted several child-initiated stories. These include the detailed boat story by Aaron (first grade) and the many stories written by Sara (third grade). These appear in Chapter 3 and Chapter 5.

It is important to note that we introduce a number of new topics here: probability, spatial relations, talking about numbers, temperature, weight, and infinity. The infinity study in Chapter 6 demonstrates the value of promoting conceptual thinking in depth. This chapter demonstrates the diverse ways in which the children explored one intriguing concept; the importance of revisiting concepts over time; and the ways in which infinity helped the children better understand other units of study such as ecology, the universe, and time.

Finally, Chapter 7 builds on the charts we have used to synthesize each of the previous chapters. The charts highlight demonstrations of authorship, classroom contexts for mathematical learning, mathematical concepts, skills, and strategies for understanding. In this chapter, we present a model for the evaluation of mathematical literacy that is theoretically consistent with the curriculum we have been promoting throughout the book. In so doing, we highlight the complementary nature of curriculum and evaluation; the relationship between the district's curriculum and evaluation guide and the curriculum Tim develops in collaboration with his students; the ways in which Tim successfully "uncovers" mandates; and the importance of grounding evaluation and curricular decisions in an understanding of concepts and strategies. We use the topic of odd and even numbers to show what the model for evaluation looks like in practice. This model also provides a lens through which classroom teachers can evaluate the curriculum as well as the children with whom they work. Evaluation from this perspective reflects and promotes the growth of teachers and children alike.

Acknowledgments

We would like to begin by thanking Devin and Colin, the best two- and three-year-old teachers we know. They show us what is possible and constantly remind us why this is important work.

Paula Mills, a devoted mother and public school activist, greatly influenced this manuscript. She touched this piece by telling her own stories—stories that portrayed "what is" and her vision of "what could be or should be" in elementary education. She did so by sharing incidents from her own children's school experiences and her personal attempts to support change at the classroom, school, and district levels. Her stories helped us envision the kind of book that would foster the development of meaningful mathematics instruction. Thank you, Paula.

We would also like to recognize the parents and children whom Tim had the privilege of teaching and whose voices ring throughout this book. He always acknowledges the children with whom he works as his greatest teachers. He now adds their parents to his list. They have been tremendously supportive of their own children's growth and, in so doing, have helped him grow personally and professionally.

We also extend our sincere appreciation to Phyllis Whitin, who helped us refine and extend the ideas of this book.

We want to express our gratitude for clerical assistance to Joyce Crosby and Lonzena Williams at the University of South Carolina. As usual, they were simultaneously patient and productive.

Of course, the folks at Heinemann cheerfully and professionally pushed us and this manuscript through the process. It was especially satisfying to work with Leigh Peake. We appreciate her insights and positive stance toward our work and the work of classroom teachers and university professors for whom this book is written. Renée Nicholls was extremely efficient and attentive to all of the details that were necessary to publish this in a short period of time. Thank you, Renée.

Finally, we want to express our genuine appreciation to Virginia Looney, for without her we can honestly say that this book would not have been written. She attended to our children, Devin and Colin, with such care that we could devote time to this project confident that they were thriving in her hands. We are truly grateful, Ginny.

From Resting to Exploring: The New Direction in Mathematics Education

This is Curtis (Figure 1–1). He has just been in an accident. It was not a serious accident, but it was an accident nonetheless. He decided to go down the playground slide headfirst. As he trudged inside with a slightly scraped forehead and a head full of sand, Mrs. Pees, the classroom tutor, began to clean away the dirt. No sooner had she begun the scrubbing

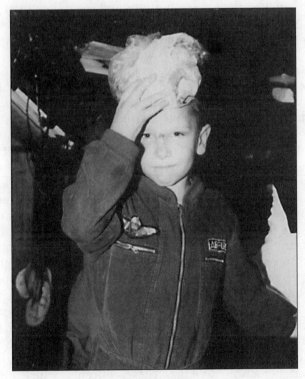

FIGURE 1–1

when Curtis turned to her and declared, "You know, I'm going to do a survey tomorrow on bruises."

"Oh you are?" said Mrs. Pees, a bit surprised that he was already thinking about a survey for tomorrow when he looked so disheveled today. "And what are you going to ask your friends in the survey?" she asked, wiping away further streaks of dirt from his forehead.

"I'm going to ask them if they think some bruises hurt or some bruises don't. I think more people is going to say they think bruises hurt," he explained.

"And what are you going to say?" inquired Mrs. Pees.

"I think they don't hurt," he said. And then, to explain his feat in more detail, he remarked, "I flew off the slide like a penguin," stretching both arms wide to demonstrate his launched position.

Although bruised and battered, Curtis was thinking like a mathematician. He viewed mathematics as a tool for collecting and analyzing information so he could answer a question that was important for him. He saw mathematics not as a way of behaving but as a way of living. It was not a stagnant system of rules and regulations but a living tool that learners use to pose their own questions and solve their own problems. From this perspective Curtis was truly an author of mathematical ideas. He was viewing the world through the mathematical concepts of equality, inequality, and quantity by predicting the survey results of his peers. It is this kind of conceptual understanding that must lie at the heart of any mathematics curriculum because thinking mathematically is embedded in concepts (Steen 1990; Bishop 1991). "Mathematicians are interested more in general concepts than in specific calculations, seeking in fact to formulate rules that can apply to the widest possible range of problems" (Gardner 1983, p. 135). Concepts are not facts, skills, or operations, but underlying generalizations that can be realized in many different ways (Burke 1991) (Table 1–1). Concepts are like lenses that learners put on to view the world in a particular way. Strategies are planful ways to solve one's problems, such as Curtis estimating the results of his possible survey; he might then use the strategies of counting and comparing to analyze his results. Skills, however, involve operational tasks to carry out those plans. Curtis, for example, might use the skill of subtracting a two-digit number from a one-digit number to help him compare his classmates' responses. Unfortunately, mathematics education has had a long history of focusing too much instructional time on skills and very little time on concepts and strategies. However, if we are to foster the development of a citizenry that is mathematically literate (NCTM 1989), we must be guided by these more global concepts for mathematical thinking. These concepts, which provide the

Table 1–1

Concepts	Strategies	Skills
equivalence, base, symmetry, probability, area, congruence, length, time, average, ratio, progression	counting, measuring, estimating, partitioning, matching, comparing, classifying, using deductive logic, noting patterns, simplifying a problem, working backwards	subtracting a one-digit number from a two-digit number; calculating the area of a rectangle; telling time to the nearest half hour

"knowledge frame," ought to be the "foci of concern, approached through activities in rich environmental contexts, explored for their mathematical meaning, logic, and connectedness, and generalized to other contexts to exemplify and validate their explanatory power" (Bishop 1991, p. 100).

This book is the story of how Curtis and some other first-, second-, and third-grade children were supported in using mathematical concepts in various contexts. At the end of each chapter is a list of concepts, strategies, and contexts that helps to demonstrate how they viewed a variety of situations from a mathematical perspective. We also have chosen to use the metaphor of authorship to describe the actions and intentions of these children because, as authors, they were encouraged to be creators of their own ideas. We use this metaphor of authorship throughout the book because it conveys for us the active, constructive, exploratory role that children must assume if they are to be the empowered mathematical thinkers that we know they can be. However, before the stories of these children unfold, it is important to understand where we have come from in the fields of reading, writing, and mathematics so we can better appreciate where we are going. The reflections of the following two students, a first grader and an eighth grader, demonstrate the problems that have been an unfortunate part of our past.

Where We Have Been

Six-year-old Rebecca entered school as an eager reader and writer. She heard many stories read aloud at home and had begun to read aloud some of these same stories to herself and to other members of her family.

She was also respected as a writer from the very beginning; she was encouraged to write her own thank-you letters and personal notes to family members, create her own stories, and record necessary items on the shopping list. Although at first her writing did not look conventional from an adult's perspective, it did hold meaning for her and it did continue to change over time as she kept taking risks as a reader and writer. However, when she entered first grade her feelings began to change. She became angry and frustrated as a writer because she had to sit through endless lessons of forming letters. During a family journal time at home, Rebecca expressed her indignation in the work (see Figure 1–2).

She labels herself and her friend Rachel as two of the students who are in the audience. She titles her paper "Boring" and writes beside her name "V4" to indicate the unit she was in at school. She was required to write this designation on all her school papers and so she includes it on this piece as well. Her piece then reads, "It is boring at school. Circle *A* 'cause it's the first letter in the alphabet. 15 minutes to wait!" To emphasize her frustration she read aloud the last line in a very sarcastic tone of voice. At home, Rebecca loved to write; she wanted to write. Her major focus was always on ideas and meaning; now what mattered was forming her letters correctly. This switch in priorities did not make sense to her. She wanted to get on with the business of really writing. It is a sad irony that she used a whole piece of writing in her journal to complain about a drill and practice exercise that was designed to teach her how to write.

In another classroom Dale Anderson was discussing mathematics with her eighth-grade students. She had just read aloud *Tom Fox and the Apple Pie* (1972) by Clyde Watson. It is the story of a fox who wants to eat an entire apple pie by himself but realizes he may have to share it with some of his friends. He imagines the pie being sliced into two, four, eight, and sixteen pieces. He realizes the size of each piece is getting smaller and smaller and so talks himself into eating the entire pie before the story ends. The children enjoyed the story and said it helped them gain a better understanding of how fractions are recorded. Amy explained her insight in this way: "I wish my teacher had read math books to me. That's the first time I've ever really understood why the smaller bottom number is worth more (i.e., why $1/2$ is greater than $1/5$, even though *5* is greater than *2*) Are there any more books that teach math? I learn better that way." It was Amy's comment that prompted others to discuss their past experiences in mathematics. Many had developed a strong distaste for mathematics during their elementary school years.

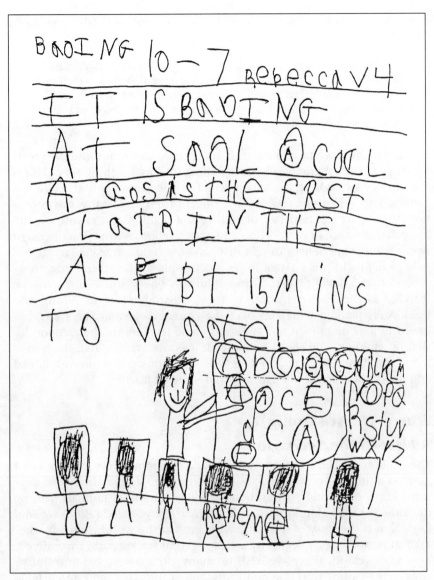

FIGURE 1–2

John captured the group's sentiments when he shared the following reflection:

> All of my teachers in elementary school always used math class as their resting time. Teachers get tired or they needed to grade papers and so they need math class to rest. They didn't show you anything like you do. They just told you to study the examples from the book and get to work. Then they sat down to rest.

And so here we have an eighth grader who saw math time as a resting time and a first grader who saw writing time as a waiting time. This is the sad news of where we have been. The good news is that we're not waiting and we're not resting any longer. There are many classrooms now that reject the passivity of resting and waiting and encourage the more active stance of exploration and conversation. A brief description of two learning experiences from a first- and a second-grade classroom will help to highlight this change in perspective about the teaching/learning process that is taking place. Throughout this book Tim O'Keefe will be featured as the teacher in both of these classrooms. David Whitin and Heidi Mills worked with Tim over the course of several years and followed him as he moved to a different grade level in another school. By sharing episodes from both of these classrooms, we are able to show a range of different-aged children, as well as demonstrate some widespread and universal processes of learning that unite all learners.

Where We Are Going

A First-Grade Scenario

The children in Tim's transition first-grade classroom were involved in a unit on animals. They had read books together, shared their own personal knowledge, and written books about a variety of animals. During this time we read aloud to his children *How Many Snails?* (1988) by Paul Giganti. It is the story of someone who looks at the world from a mathematical perspective. It begins by asking, "I went walking and I wondered, how many clouds there were? How many clouds were big and fluffy? How many clouds were big and fluffy and gray?" This same predictable story structure runs throughout the book as the reader walks through meadows; visits lakes, libraries, and bakeries; and wonders about flowers, fish, books, and cupcakes. The author poses three questions on each page that encourage readers to count each group of objects according to different attributes. Toward the end of the story there is a picture of a toy store that is filled with miniature trucks, cars, buses, and boats. After the children answered questions posed by the author such as, "How many trucks there were? How many trucks were fire trucks? How many trucks were fire trucks and had ladders on them?" they began to pose their own questions quite spontaneously. Marques began the discussion and others followed his lead:

MARQUES: We could say, how many planes?

AMANDA: How many small cars?

CHARLES: How many dump trucks?

KAREEM: How many boats?

DERRICK: How many people in the cars?

After each person posed a question, the rest of the class counted together to find the answer. When we had finished reading the story we invited the children to create their own class book using this same story structure. Since they had been studying animals we asked them to draw their own set of animals and then pose some questions about that group. Justin began by drawing a variety of animals: "How many live in the water? How many eat bugs? Who goes the fastest? Skunk, fox, snake, snail, owl."

At the top of his paper he wrote his first question, "How many live in the water?" When the class asked him to justify his answer of two, he remarked, "There is the snail. And the snake does too. He lives in the swamp." He was also intrigued with the speed of animals and so wrote above the picture of his skunk, "Who goes the fastest?" There was a chart posted in the classroom about the speed of animals and Justin consulted this chart to answer his own question. He wrote "40" next to the owl to indicate that the owl was the fastest animal in his set, capable of traveling up to forty mph. He also consulted another chart in the room that listed the longevity of animals and wrote "24" next to the owl as well, saying, "That's how long it lives."

Jessica saw Justin using these animal charts and decided to incorporate a similar question on her own paper: "Who lives the longest? How many have legs? How many have fur? Spider, snake, panda, cat, bunny rabbit." Above the spider she wrote, "Who lives the longest?" She also included some additional questions, "How many have legs?" and "How many have fur?" Tony was also interested in counting legs and posed two questions that related to this attribute: "How many animals have eight legs? How many swallow their food whole? How many have zero legs?" (Figure 1–3). He drew a spider, snake, cat and bear. Above the spider he wrote, "How many animals have eight legs?" After he read his question aloud he glanced at this drawing and realized his mistake. "Oh, no! I put sixteen legs on the spider. I forgot!" He had been so intent on making legs to go all around the spider that he did not bother to count them. On the far right side of his paper he posed another question about legs: "How many have zero legs?" In Tony's set of animals, the attribute of having "zero legs" was unique to snakes, and Tony enjoyed posing it as one of his questions. Obviously snakes were one of Tony's favorite animals, and so his third question also

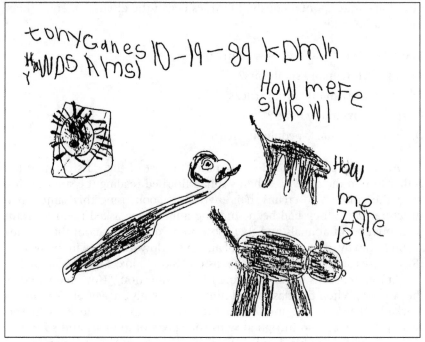

FIGURE 1–3

captured a special characteristic of this reptile, "How many swallow their food whole?"

Paul expanded the range of questions by asking even further, "How many hop? How many crawl on the ground? How many lay eggs? Bird, bug, spider." He posed two questions that focused on how animals move (in the lower left corner): "How many hop? How many crawl on the ground?" Below these questions he drew a series of rabbits to show their movement across the ground, and he drew a zigzag line to indicate the movement of a snake as it crawls. He also recalled one of the distinguishing contrasts between reptiles and mammals when he wrote in the lower right corner, "How many lay eggs?"

Finally, it was Jason who really wanted to pose a tricky question for his classmates to answer: "How many pigs? How many have two legs? Spider, dog, turtle, bunny, panda bear, pig, pig." At the bottom of his paper he wrote, "How many pigs? How many have two legs?" It was the second question that he hoped would stump a few of his friends. He had purposely drawn a number of animals but *none* of them walked on two legs. All of the questions in *How Many Snails?* had answers greater than zero. Jason hoped that this slight change he had created might fool some of his friends.

As we reflected on the diverse questions that children posed, we created a chart to better understand the connections they were making (Figure 1–4).

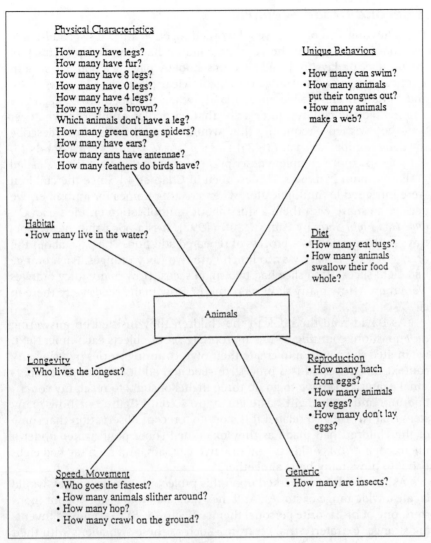

Physical Characteristics

How many have legs?
How many have fur?
How many have 8 legs?
How many have 0 legs?
How many have 4 legs?
How many have brown?
Which animals don't have a leg?
How many green orange spiders?
How many have ears?
How many ants have antennae?
How many feathers do birds have?

Unique Behaviors

• How many can swim?
• How many animals
  put their tongues out?
• How many animals
  make a web?

Habitat
• How many live in the water?

Diet
• How many eat bugs?
• How many animals
  swallow their food
  whole?

Animals

Longevity
• Who lives the longest?

Reproduction
• How many hatch
  from eggs?
• How many animals
  lay eggs?
• How many don't lay
  eggs?

Speed, Movement
• Who goes the fastest?
• How many animals slither around?
• How many hop?
• How many crawl on the ground?

Generic
• How many are insects?

FIGURE 1–4

Some chose to highlight important physical attributes such as fur, antennae, or legs; others used descriptive words to capture the variation in animal movement, such as *slither, hop,* and *crawl*; still others were interested in snakes and they posed questions that fit the unique characteristics of this animal, such as "How many animals put their tongues out? (unique behaviors), "How many animals swallow their food whole?" (diet), and "How many have zero legs?" (physical characteristics). Their questions were varied and diverse and helped to demonstrate some of the children's current understanding of animals and their distinguishing characteristics.

A Second-Grade Scenario

The following school year we all worked together in Tim's second-grade classroom. Throughout the year the children had been keeping track of the number of days they had been in school by placing a popsicle stick in a "ones" bag every morning. They had a clear plastic bag for ones, tens, and hundreds and traded appropriately when the need arose. Each day Tim invited the children to describe that particular number in whatever way they wished. Frequently they would use multiplication to describe the daily number, such as $(2 \times 25) + 13 = 63$, or $(6 \times 10) + 3 = 63$, or $(4 \times 15) + 3 = 63$. (A more complete description of this strategy, which we called "Talking About Numbers," is described in Chapter 4.) Since the children were intrigued by multiplication when creating names for a number, we decided to share with them a story about multiplication entitled *Each Orange Had Eight Slices* by Paul Giganti (1992). It is a book that nicely portrays multiplication as a process of repeated addition. The page about the orange reads, "On my way to lunch I ate two juicy oranges. Each orange had eight slices. Each slice had two small seeds. How many juicy oranges were there? How many slices were there? How many seeds were there in all?"

As David read the book to the children they insisted on answering *each* question, counting by the appropriate set of objects each time. Next, we invited the children to create their own counting stories by using any context that reflected this process of repeated addition. Tim gave a personal example, "I have to go up three flights of stairs to reach my condominium, and each flight has eight steps. I could figure out how many steps that is." He also related this story to a recent observation that some of the children had made as they examined some pond water under a microscope, "You could say you saw two egg sacs, and each sac had eight hairs, so how many hairs altogether?"

As the children embarked upon this project we predicted they would create a wide range of stories. And they did. Alex told a story about monsters, one of his favorite personal themes (Figure 1–5). He enjoyed inventing strange, extraterrestrial creatures, such as these two aliens with their two bodies, three heads, four eyes, and five pupils! His story reflects a factorial sequence of numbers: $1 \times 2 = 2$ bodies, $1 \times 2 \times 3 = 6$ heads, $1 \times 2 \times 3 \times 4 = 24$ eyes, and $1 \times 2 \times 3 \times 4 \times 5 = 120$ pupils. Earlier in the year we had read to the class *Anno's Mysterious Multiplying Jar* by Anno (1983) in which there is one jar containing two islands, with three mountains per island, four castles per mountain, and so on. Alex cleverly tied these two pieces of literature together and then wrote his own story that highlighted this special sequence of multiplying numbers. He loved using large numbers and finding patterns in numbers; his story shows this interest.

There was 1 Monster, that had two bodys, that had three heads, that had four eyes that had five puples!!!

How many body's?
How many head's?
How many eyes?
How many puples?

Puple's 120
body's 2
eye's 24
Head's 6

FIGURE 1–5

Other children tied their stories to a familiar classroom theme: *The Wizard of Oz* (Baum 1993). Tim had read aloud several books in this series and the children had become enthralled with these characters and their adventures. Larry wrote a mathematical story that included the four main characters: "There were 4 Oz characters. Each one had 2 eyes and each one of them had 2 arms and 2 legs. How many eyes are altogether? How many legs are all together? How many arms are altogether? How many arms and legs and eyes are there altogether?" He drew a key in the upper left corner of his paper to show which particular body parts needed to be counted.

Two other children wrote about the Oz characters but focused on the patchwork girl. Ashley wrote, "Once there was a patchwork girl. She had 30 patches. Each patch had 20 dots. How many in all?" Although she had created a multiplication story, she was not sure how to solve it. David asked her to draw a picture of her problem; she drew thirty squares, wrote "20" inside each one, and then counted by twenties to one hundred six times, giving her a total of six hundred dots. Thus, Ashley posed a problem for herself that challenged her thinking. It made sense to her because it was tied to a subject she was familiar with and she solved it by illustrating and counting the patches. Andy also wrote a story about the patchwork girl but he focused on the concept of money (Figure 1–6). He always enjoyed calculating monetary sums and his story certainly reflects

1 pachwork girl

2 shose

each shoe had 10 rubys

each ruby was worth 37,000$ Dolors

How much money in all?

740,000

FIGURE 1–6

that interest. He used several attributes for his calculation, just as Giganti's story had done: the two shoes contained ten rubies each, and each ruby was worth thirty-seven thousand dollars. He created an interesting two-step problem for his classmates to solve.

Several children looked around the room for examples of repeated addition. Andrea cleverly used the bowls of crayons that children used throughout the year. She wrote, "6 crayon bowls. Each bowl had 15 crayons. Each crayon had 7 letters. (1) How many crayons? (2) How many letters?" She had actually counted the number of letters in the word *Crayola* to be sure her story was accurate. She also noted that her drawings did not show all fifteen crayons in each bowl but explained, "Some of them are inside the bowl. You just can't see them." Andrea created another story that involved the cabinets she saw in the classroom:

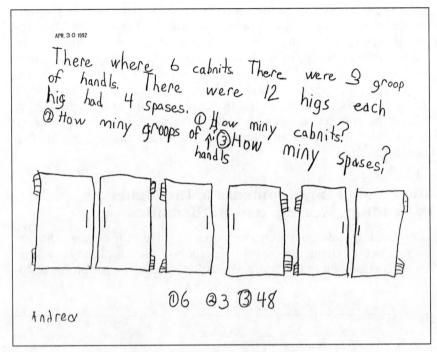

APR. 3 0 1992

FIGURE 1–7

"There were 6 cabinets. There were 3 groups of handles. There were 12 hinges. Each hinge had 4 spaces. (1) How many cabinets? (2) How many groups of handles? (3) How many spaces?" (Figure 1–7). In both stories she used the familiar context of the classroom to write some interesting mathematical stories.

Brittany noticed that the cover of the library book on her desk showed a three by five array of fifteen cubbies. She imagined a lunchbox in each cubby and wrote, "Everybody had in their lunchboxes two cheeseburgers. How many in all? 30 cheeseburgers." Abby used a familiar object from the kitchen: "I have a toaster and there are 2 holes in my toaster, 2 waffles in each hole. (1) How many waffles? (2) How many holes? (3) How many toasters?"

Becky's love of horses was revealed in her story: "There were 10 horses. Each horse had 1 groomer. And each horse had infinity hairs. And each horse had 2 ears, 2 eyes, 2 nostrils, 1 mouth and 2 whiskers." The concept of infinity had become a classroom theme (see Chapter 6 for a more complete description of infinity) and Becky incorporated it into her story. She contrasted body parts that can be easily counted with hairs that are too numerous to count. Kyle also reflects his love of animal life in his story: "There were 4 fish. Each fish had 11 teeth. Each tooth had 2 cavities. How many teeth and cavities together?" (Figure 1–8). Thus, the open-ended nature of this classroom invitation supported learners to tie this process of multiplication to other pieces of literature (*Anno's Mysterious Multiplying Jar, The Land of Oz, The Patchwork Girl of Oz*), objects in the room (crayons, cabinet doors, cubbies), personal themes of interest (monsters, horses, and fish), and the class theme of infinity. Each story reflects the context of repeated addition through a variety of contexts. Reading and writing became important tools for exploring this mathematical situation.

The Parallel Developments in the Fields of Reading, Writing, and Mathematics

The preceding classroom scenarios help to highlight the changes that are taking place in elementary school classrooms. The education profession has reached a point in time now where there is clearly a parallel develop-

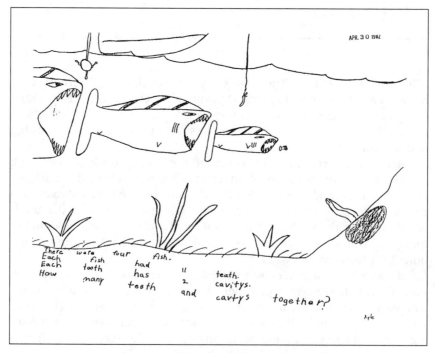

FIGURE 1–8

ment in the fields of reading, writing, and mathematics. *Curriculum and Evaluation Standards for School Mathematics*, recently published by the National Council of Teachers of Mathematics (1989), is certainly consistent with the major emphases in the fields of reading and writing. Some of the major characteristics of this parallel development are (1) a process perspective, (2) an emphasis on functionality, (3) valuing sense over symbol, (4) supporting alternative communication systems, and (5) the importance of the social dimension of learning.

Let's discuss some of the strands of this parallel development in more detail and see how it relates to the classroom scenarios that were just described.

A Process Perspective

There is a movement away from a skills approach to learning that isolates and fragments reading, writing, and mathematics into artificially controlled situations. The movement is toward a transactive model of learning that seeks to understand the meaning-making processes of learners as they use reading, writing, and mathematics for real purposes. There is an increasing emphasis on *how* children learn. In the previous first-grade classroom scenario, Justin and Jessica demonstrated how they were learning by using the class animal charts on speed and longevity to pose their own questions. In the second-grade scenario, Brittany strategically used the cover of her library book to give her an idea for a classroom story while Alex tied two pieces of literature together to help him create his own story. They all were showing themselves to be flexible problem solvers who identified and used classroom resources appropriately.

An Emphasis on Functionality

There is an emphasis on the functionality of reading, writing, and mathematics in that they are tools for learning and not merely ends in themselves. It is in this context that Frank Smith (1988) describes the importance of a "literacy club"—a community of language users who are admitted to the club from the very beginning. Even though they cannot read or write conventionally they are nevertheless supported by more experienced members who encourage them to participate in meaningful literacy endeavors. The National Council of Teachers of Mathematics (1989) argues that this perspective toward learning can be applied to the development of mathematical literacy as well. Learners best understand mathematics as they use it purposefully in various situations. In Tim's first-grade classroom the children used a variety of mathematical concepts in an authentic way, such as the concept of time ("Who goes the fastest?" and "Who lives the longest?"), the concept of quantity ("How many have eight legs? no legs? four legs?"), and the concept of sets ("How many hatch their eggs?" and "How many swallow their food whole?"). In this way the children used mathematical concepts in a purposeful manner to communicate some important differences among the animals they chose to represent. In the second-grade classroom the children incorporated the concepts of money, quantity, infinity, and a factorial to tell their stories. When the experience is open ended, children will weave these concepts together in interesting ways.

Valuing Sense over Symbol

In the fields of reading, writing, and mathematics, children are viewed as sense-makers, not mistake-makers (Lampert 1986). Although children's early attempts at talking may sound like nonsense, any parent can tell you that their children are trying to communicate a request, a feeling, or an idea. These early attempts at talking may sound unconventional, but they are based on thinking that is logical, systematic, and rule governed. Thus the role of conventions, whether they be grammar rules or mathematical symbols, are only important in their larger role of supporting meaning. As children write messages, stories, and science observations, or as they construct a graph or measure some objects, teachers value the learners' intentions. The children in the first-grade classroom scenario used reading, writing, mathematics, and art to communicate important characteristics of animals. When Jessica wrote *A M E I V V R* ("How many have fur?") and Paul wrote *H Y M N I A E Z* ("How many lay eggs?"), they demonstrated their understanding of distinguishing animal attributes and their current knowledge of the sound/symbol relationships. When Justin wrote "40" and "24" next to his drawing of an owl and then read those numbers as "That's how fast it goes" and "That's how long it lives," he demonstrated that he knows numbers can placehold the ideas of speed and longevity. The point is that although some of their written symbols do not look conventional, they are intentional; they are written by learners who use them purposefully to placehold important ideas. This is the sense that must come first in the process of learning the symbol.

Supporting Alternative Communication Systems

Learners need increasing opportunities to represent their ideas through a variety of communication systems. Oral and written language, drama, music, art, mathematics, and so on are all important channels for representing ideas. Instructional invitations that allow students to use art, mathematics, and written language in concert and share meaning provide opportunities to create new thoughts as well as new ways to think. For instance, in the previous first-grade classroom scenario Paul drew a series of rabbits to convey the movement of hopping and a zigzag line to show the movement of a snake along the ground. The jagged line and the repetition of rabbits helped show how art could be used to show movement in two different ways. Paul was helping all of us think in a new way about the movement of animals; he was helping us think through the eyes of an artist. In the second-grade classroom, Alex used his drawing of monsters to convey effectively the power of a factorial sequence while Andrea used a series of bowls of crayons to demonstrate the process of repeated addition. Art helps to support the mathematical stories these children had created.

Social Dimension of Learning

Learning is a social process (Barnes 1987; Vygotsky 1938/1978). In the fields of reading, writing, and mathematics, there is a call for the development of classrooms that are communities of learners where all participants are both teachers and learners and where all voices are heard and respected (Watson, Burke, and Hartse 1989). From a mathematical perspective, these are classrooms where statistical information is challenged, not merely manipulated; conclusions are questioned, not merely drawn; and problems are posed, not merely solved. When we read aloud *How Many Snails?* to the first-grade children they became intrigued by the page depicting transportation vehicles and began to pose their own questions. The discussion demonstrated how a learning community can generate new knowledge together.

Another aspect of the social dimension of learning is that learners can provide demonstrations for each other about their own learning process. Justin demonstrated to Jessica the usefulness of the animal charts on speed and longevity; Jessica then used this resource to pose her own question of "Who lives the longest?" The social nature of learning also implies that learners have a sense of audience. Certainly Jason showed us this aspect of the learning process when he tried to create a tricky question for his friends to answer. In the second-grade classroom the children discussed with each other possible topics for writing; although some used the same themes, such as the Oz character, they used that theme in their own way. They supported each other in finding topics that reflected this counting pattern of repeated addition.

These are some of the common features of the parallel development in the fields of reading, writing, and mathematics. Their implications for the teaching/learning process can be summarized in the following table (1–2):

Table 1–2

Parallel Strands	Curricular Implications	Attitudinal Implications
Process Perspective	Value how children think by giving them time to share their learning strategies	I can grow as a learner when I take time to reflect on how I learn.
Functionality	Provide demonstrations for learners so that they come to understand the real purposes of reading, writing, and mathematics	I can learn about reading, writing, and mathematics as I see other people use it.
Sense over Symbol	Focus on the intentions of learners as they construct and share meaning	I can use reading, writing, and mathematics as tools for learning.
Alternative Communication Systems	Provide learners with continual opportunities to represent their ideas through different communication systems	I have many choices in how I represent my ideas.
Social Nature of Learning	Provide learners time to converse and share with others	I can view my own thinking in different ways when others share their own perspectives with me.

Learning as Authoring

The parallel development in the fields of reading, writing, and mathematics calls for a different role for learners in the classroom. No longer are children seen as passive receivers of knowledge; they are respected as active constructors of their own knowledge. Teachers are learners, too, as they value children's thinking strategies and plan curricular invitations that are consistent with their theory of how people learn best. From this perspective children and teachers can be viewed as authors in the classroom. Authoring is really a synonym for learning (Short, Harste, and Burke 1995), and it nicely captures in a single word the most significant features of this parallel development. Although we often use the word *author* to describe what readers and writers do, we can also use this same term to describe what mathematicians do as well. Let's view two other classroom experiences that help to show how this metaphor of authorship is acted out.

Investigating Foot Size in a First-Grade Classroom

The children in Tim's transition first-grade classroom had been collecting and displaying information about themselves for some time. They found the height and weight of each person in the class and showed their results on large charts that they posted in the hallway. On this particular day in February we brought to class a device for measuring shoe sizes, known as a shoe braddick. It was a piece of plastic in the shape of a large shoe that a local shoe store had donated to the classroom. We thought that such a tool might extend their interest in measuring. As the children came to school that morning, we asked them to find their foot size and then write their name under the appropriate number on the board. Together, we obtained the following results:

12	13	14	15	16	17	18	19	20
Le Ann	Jessica	Chiquita	Stephen	Chris	Mrs. Pees		David	Mr. O'Keefe
Nathan	Megan		Charles	Marques				
Amanda	Tony		Heidi	Michael				
Jason	Nikkie							
	Vania							
	Justin							
	Kareem							

During the morning gathering time the children interpreted the results. First of all, Tony extended the exploration by suggesting, "Let's do the grown-ups." Tim, Heidi, David and Mrs. Pees (the classroom aide) then placed their results on the chart. When Vania saw the results of the grown-ups, she noted a unique relationship:

15	16	17	18	19	20
Heidi		Mrs. Pees		David	Mr. O'Keefe

"It's like a pattern," she said. "It's got a number [15], nothing there [16], got a number [17], then there's nothing there [18], and if you take Mr.

O'Keefe off there would be a pattern." She nicely described the (almost) alternating sequence of names. Many children documented comparisons:

> "Marques and Michael have 16."
> "Charles and Stephen have the same foot."
> "Heidi has a small foot like Stephen and Charles."
> "Kareem and Tony are the same."
> "Heidi is like a little kid 'cause her foot is small."

They also made some more general statements:

> "Mostly everyone has 13 'cause most everyone has little feet."
> "Some people have 12 'cause their feet are smaller."

We left the shoe braddick available for other children to use during the morning work time. Vania decided to use the tool to collect the data again but she chose to represent her findings in a different way (Figure 1–9). However, she went through several revisions before she decided upon the format shown in Figure 1–9. She drew the numbers on the left-hand side of her paper first and began to draw a small foot next to each number to indicate each person's size. However, she abandoned that strategy because she was not satisfied with the way she drew the feet. Next, she began to write the names of people next to their appropriate numeral, but she discarded that strategy as well because "If I write the names on here, I wouldn't have enough space [and she points to the thirteen column where there are seven names], and I would have to use another line, and people would think the names go with 14." So she tallied the number of respondees for each size and wrote that total with a single digit. When we asked her how her representation of the data differed from the representation on the chalkboard, she said, "You can see the numbers more easily on mine and I put the arrows to the number so you could put the numbers together." In this way Vania created a visual that highlighted more clearly the numerical results of the group at the expense of individual identities. It was an important distinction to make. Neither was right nor wrong, merely different. And since the representation of the data was different, it offered new possibilities for interpretation. When Vania looked at her visual and discussed her results, she made many purely numerical observations:

"If you put all these together [$1 + 1 + 1 + 3 + 3 + 1$] it's ten."
"And if you put seven and four together it's eleven."
"There's two that have three kids, [columns] 15 and 16."

Justin also wanted to survey people about their foot size. He traced around the perimeter of the braddick as Vania had done, but then placed his number line in the center of that outline as it actually appeared on the measuring tool (Figure 1–10). He, too, was concerned that he might not have enough room for writing all the names next to the appropriate

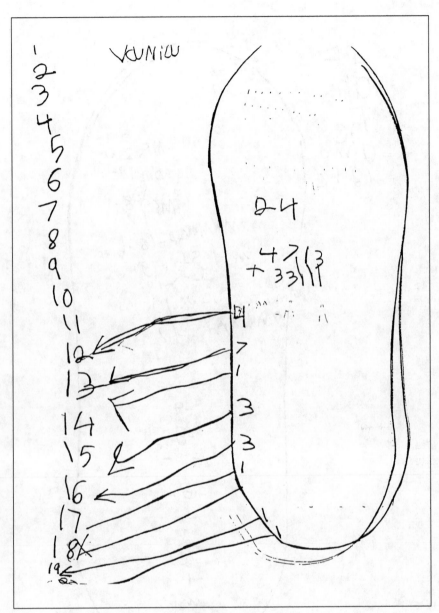

FIGURE 1–9

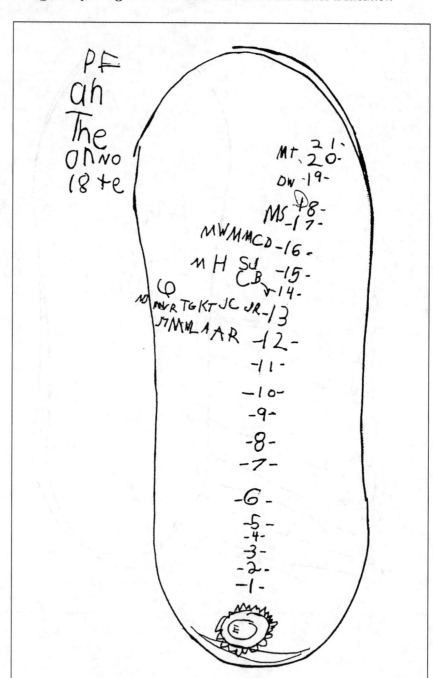

FIGURE 1–10

numbers, so he decided to use only initials. He also wrote some interesting interpretations of his data in the left-hand corner of his paper: "Paul Finch ain't here. There ain't no [column] 18."

When Justin and Vania shared their visual representations with the class, the children contributed additional interpretations from those they had offered initially. Jason noted, "Everybody is up here," and Chiquita said, "Nobody has these numbers" (pointing to the columns 1 through 11). These observations described general trends in the data; the children could better see the general shape of the data and how the names clustered together at the upper part of the scale. The lack of names next to columns *1* through *11* also generated a brief debate about the shoe size of infants:

"A baby has one."

"No, a baby would have six."

"No, four."

"No, eleven."

The first representation of the data that we made on the blackboard did not show the 1 through 11 range of numbers as only sizes 12 through 20 were represented. However, Vania and Justin included this range in their representations. Even though no names were listed next to this lower range, the very absence of names interested the children and provided them the opportunity to discuss the data in another way.

The children were also invited to bring the shoe braddick home and collect information from family members. When Amanda shared her results with the class she demonstrated still another way to represent her findings. She explained, "I wanted to put these dots to show that I left space." In this way she used dots rather than the horizontal lines on the foot device to show the spacing between each number. She also explained, "I went up to these numbers so they can know what they got— my mom, and Alex, and my dad." Thus, the sheer quantity of numbers that she wrote under each name helped to distinguish the smaller sizes from the larger ones.

Investigating Foot Size in a Second-Grade Classroom

Another example of thinking mathematically involved the investigation by Andy, a student in Tim's second-grade classroom. He had walked up to his friend Kyle one day and noticed that they were the same height. He asked his friend, "Hey, what size shoe do you wear?" When Kyle responded "Three," Andy ventured the following hypothesis: "I think people who are the same height have same shoe size." As Andy shared this idea with his teacher, they brainstormed some other possible relationships to pursue, such as, "If you have the same shoe size, do you have the same cubit length?" (a nonstandard unit of measure that the children had used previously; see Chapter 4 for additional information) and, "If you have the same shoe size, do you have the same head circumference?" They wondered further, "If two people are the same height, what else might be the same about them? What might be different?" Thus, Andy's initial hypothesis generated a host of other relationships to consider. He was thinking mathematically because he was thinking through concepts. He was using the concept of length to investigate a relationship that was interesting to him.

Andy looked at the chart of classmates' names on the wall and copied the first few letters of each person's name onto his own chart (Figure 1–11). He divided his recording sheet into two sections, the upper portion representing height and the lower portion representing shoe size.

As Andy began to collect his data he discovered that everyone either knew their shoe size or could find it by looking inside their sneakers. However, few people knew their exact height, so he decided to forget that piece of data for the moment. As he began to collect the shoe size data, some of the results did not make sense to him. He began to notice that some of the tallest girls in the class did not have as large a shoe size as some of the boys of comparable height. As he shared this anomaly with his classmates, some suggested that perhaps there are different sizes for girls and boys. Although neither the children nor the adults in the room were quite sure about this possible explanation, Andy felt that this reasoning was probably true. With this additional piece of information in mind he created another visual representation of his data (Figure 1–12), subdividing the class into sets of girls and boys so he could make comparisons only within these two categories.

After Andy divided the class into girls and boys, he recorded their shoe sizes beneath their names. He then looked within each category to find people with the same shoe size and had them stand back-to-back to see if they were the same height. There are several important points to make here about his problem-solving efforts. First, he found a way to investigate his hypothesis without actually having to measure the height of each person. He was thinking mathematically by utilizing the strategy of comparing to solve his problem in an efficient way. Second, because people did not know their own heights, he explored the conditions of his hypothesis in reverse order. Originally he had proposed, "If you're the same height, you have the same shoe size." Now he was hypothesizing, "If you have the same shoe size, then you will be the same height." Andy did not allow the original wording of his hypothesis to interfere with his unique method for exploring it.

He found on his chart that Christopher and Kyle had the same shoe size. He drew a line to connect these two names and then had them stand back-to-back. He had predicted that they would be the same height; when he found that they were not, he realized he had to show this unanticipated result in some way. "I know," he said, "I'll make an *x* to show they aren't

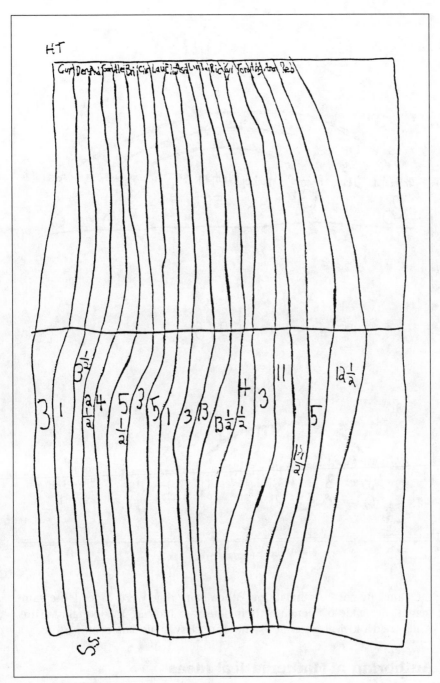

FIGURE 1–11

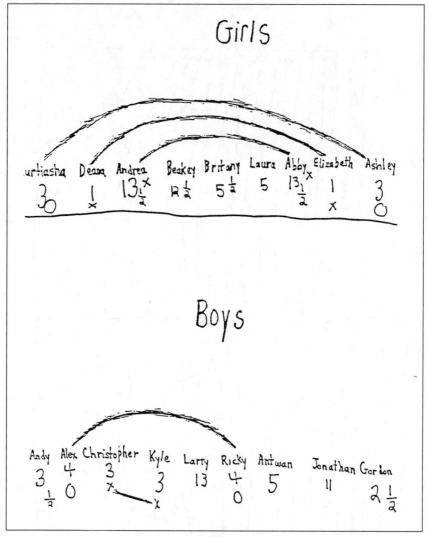

FIGURE 1–12

the same height." As he found other pairs that were indeed the same height, he made o's beneath their names to indicate this equality. Thus, Andy used a logical system of symbols to classify his data even further.

Authoring of Mathematical Ideas

We began this chapter with a boy named Curtis. He had traveled down the playground slide headfirst and had received a few cuts and bruises.

Even as the sand and dirt was being wiped from his forehead he was thinking like an author of mathematical ideas. He knew he wanted to gather quantitative information about his experience by asking his classmates if they thought bruises hurt, and he was also predicting his results: "I think more people is going to say they think bruises hurt." Curtis was using the concepts of quantity and inequality to frame his recent mishap on the playground. Seeing the world through mathematical concepts made Curtis an author of mathematical ideas.

The rest of Curtis's first-grade classmates who were involved in measuring each other's foot size were also authors of their own learning (a summary of these authoring characteristics is found in Table 1–3).

Like Curtis, they saw themselves as full-fledged members of the literacy club; they were using mathematics for real purposes. They had already weighed and measured each other and wanted to use the foot braddick to gather further information. This measuring experience built upon interests the children had already expressed; in this way the

Table 1–3   Authors in the Mathematics Classroom

Characteristics of Authors	Mathematical Implications	Attitudinal Implications
They write about what they know.	Develop learning experiences that build on their interests	They come to value their own experiences and view them as assets for learning.
They share texts with others.	Provide time for learners to share problems, stories, and strategies with each other	They see each other as having strengths and resources that are to be valued.
They use alternative communication systems to reflect and extend meaning.	Encourage learners to draw, write, discuss, and dramatize what they know	They view themselves as learners with a wide range of options.
They initiate their own investigations.	Encourage learners to record their own discoveries and explorations	They view themselves as makers of their own ideas.
They grow through prolonged engagements in the process.	Provide learners extended periods of time to solve problems and explore patterns	They see themselves as thinkers, not doers, of mathematics.
They reflect and revise.	Support learners to test out different ways to solve problems	They view themselves as questioners and problem posers.

children were coming to see themselves as authors who had unique experiences that were assets for learning. Andy, too, saw himself as an author of his own mathematical ideas by sharing an initial observation about his friend Kyle and then using that observation as a seed for further inquiry.

Authors are also generators of knowledge. Certainly the first-grade children's many interpretations of the data they collected was evidence of that. They also extended the investigation by suggesting, "Let's do grown-ups." Authors are always growing, and this kind of extension of the original survey is the stuff that authors are made of. Authors are inquirers and their work is never done; they are always posing fresh questions, raising new issues, offering alternative interpretations. This kind of questioning occurred later on when they began to debate the size of a baby's foot. Authors are always challenging, extending, and reshaping the data they have collected.

Authors are also risk-takers who are unafraid to try out a host of ideas because they know that there is nothing sacred about first drafts. Vania certainly demonstrated this aspect of authoring when she revised her visual representation several times so she could show her findings in the clearest way. Andy also did some revising of his own. When he noticed the inconsistency about the shoe sizes for girls and boys, he devised another way to organize his data by subdividing the class into two subsets of children. As an author he reshaped his text (his visual display of data) to better meet the inexplicable responses of his audience. Authors also know they have a wide range of options to represent their ideas. Vania, Justin, and Amanda chose their own unique way to show their findings. Vania focused on writing a numerical summary for each size while Justin used the initials of his classmates to preserve their individuality. Amanda used dots instead of horizontal lines to indicate the spacing in her measurement scale; she also created a measurement scale for each person while Vania and Justin drew a single measurement scale for the whole class. Authors are brainstormers who keep thinking of alternative ways to represent their ideas. Authors do not busy themselves by trying to label their representations as "right" or "wrong." Such labeling tends to narrow thinking and cut off conversations. Instead, they discuss the strengths and limitations of each visual representation. For instance, where the names of the adults were recorded, the children could see an alternating pattern of sizes; when the full scale of numbers was displayed, the children noted the absence of names for sizes 1 through 11 and began to conjecture about the size of a baby's foot. It is this weighing of strengths and limitations that expands thinking and generates new conversations. Authors are always eager to enter new conversations.

As authors the children were also engaged in mathematical thinking (Table 1–4). They viewed a variety of mathematical concepts—such as quantity, equivalence, and length—across contexts such as responding to

Table 1–4 Reflecting on These Mathematical Experiences

Demonstrations of Authorship	Classroom Context	Mathematical Concept	Strategies for Understanding
Authors write about what they know.	Curtis bruises himself going down the slide.	Quantity, equality, inequality	Comparing responses of his peers
Authors write about what they know, use alternative communication systems.	Children respond to *How Many Snails?*	Quantity, time, length	Counting, classifying
Authors write about what they know, use alternative communication systems.	Children respond to *Each Orange Had Eight Slices.*	Quantity, area (a three by five array), infinity	Counting, classifying (sets of objects)
Authors initiate their own investigations, revise their texts (Vania), grow through prolonged engagements.	Collecting information about the size of their bodies	Length, quantity	Comparing, noting patterns
Authors initiate their own investigations, use alternative communication (Andy) systems.	Andy compares his own height to his friend's height.	Length	Comparing, matching

literature and measuring foot size. They accessed such strategies as counting, comparing, and classifying to help them analyze and interpret their results. We will use this framework of authorship, context, concepts, and strategies as a vehicle for summarizing the key features of the mathematical engagements of each chapter. We feel it can be a powerful way to focus on what really matters in mathematics.

Looking Ahead

This book is the story of two classrooms of children who are supported to be authors of mathematical ideas. We have devoted Chapters 2 and 4 to "Authorship Throughout the Day," which describe the context of the

learning environment in more detail so that readers can better understand how the metaphor of authorship is supported and integrated into
the daily life of these two classrooms. We have devoted Chapters 3 and 5
to individual authors—Aaron in the first grade and Sarah in the second
and third grades—so that readers might come to know and appreciate
the unique strategies demonstrated by specific children. Chapter 6, "Exploring Concepts over Time: Infinity Strikes Again," helps to show the
crucial role that concepts play in fostering a mathematical way of thinking. Chapter 7, "Rethinking Curriculum and Evaluation," takes a close
look at what really counts in the teaching and learning of mathematics
and discusses how we can begin to document and value these more important understandings we seek to foster in our classrooms. In the epi-
logue, Tim speaks directly to classroom teachers about the practical
dimensions of creating a holistic mathematics curriculum.

Authoring Throughout the Day   **2**

We devised this chapter in response to questions that teachers posed to us after reading *Living and Learning Mathematics* (Whitin, Mills, O'Keefe 1990). Teachers found the use of surveys, graphs, children's literature, and invitations built upon children's needs and interests both practical and inspiring. Yet, soon after introducing them to their children, new questions emerged. They asked,

> How does it all fit together?
>
> What does a typical day look like?
>
> I understand how to use reading and writing throughout the curriculum, but how do I weave mathematics into the fabric of classroom life?

In this chapter, we have created a portrait that captures a typical day in Tim O'Keefe's transition first-grade classroom.

Welcome to the transition first-grade classroom at R. Earle Davis Elementary School. The entire group will be featured in this chapter as we share the mathematical insights that were generated on January 31, 1989. In this chapter we portray the richly contextualized nature of learning in this community. We chose the "typical day" format to show

- connections between and across curricular experiences,
- the diverse range of mathematical events that occur in a day,
- the ways in which meanings are constructed, strategies are shared, and concepts understood,
- how the curriculum is shaped and reshaped by the participants,
- the role of mathematics in the curriculum as a tool for learning and a system for communication, and

- how the teacher attempts to understand what children know
  about mathematics and builds from there by creating open-
  ended invitations with no entry or exit prerequisites.

We hope that your vicarious visit with our class will help you construct an
authentic vision of the curriculum and learners who live and learn in it.

Morning Choices

"Don't forget to sign-in," Tray remarked in his best teacher's voice as he
walked past the cubbies. Several of his friends were busy hanging up
their coats and putting up their book bags. The attendance journal was
almost complete but Tray could tell from a glance that there were several
names missing. Reggie, Michael, and Joshua continued the animated
conversation that had begun on the playground. As they approached the
journal, however, they redirected their thinking to consider what had recently become an important issue each morning: the number of children
present and/or absent. Tray's gentle nudge had been accepted graciously.
As these three carefully inscribed their names in the sign-in journal, they
read the date and the names of the children who were already busy at
work in the classroom. Before moving on, they paused and counted each
name on the list in unison (Figure 2–1). Ongoing experiences such as the
attendance journal provided daily opportunities for the children to read
each other's names, count, compare, and make predictions about the status of the class. Attendance charts also became a regular source of data
for children to use in constructing graphs of their own design.

Reggie and Michael decided to begin playing a game together. Reggie
suggested a game created by two of their friends, Alex and Daniell. Game
making was an important feature of the curriculum. The children's
games were often quite sophisticated. This one followed the pattern of
many created by this group; it had "dangers" that required players to
move several spaces back and "rewards" that allowed players to move
ahead. In an attempt to reduce competition and encourage collaboration
there was a general class rule that the game was over when all players
were finished. This game was no exception. As they played, they helped
each other refine an effective and efficient adding strategy that they had
recently learned during a class strategy-sharing session. After rolling two
number cubes they looked for the larger number. They read the larger
number together and then added the second number by counting on until the sum was reached. Michael rolled a five and a three. "Five and six,
seven, eight!" they exclaimed to calculate the appropriate number of
spaces to move ahead (Figure 2–2).

At the same time, Tim was working with a small group of children in

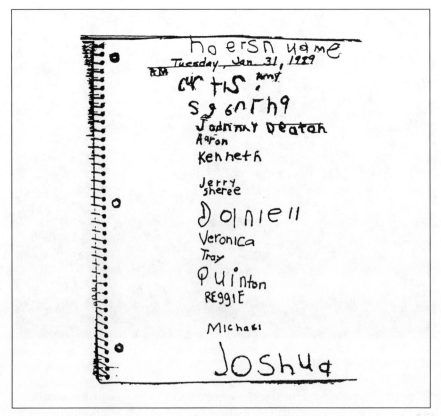

FIGURE 2–1

the science area. They were writing observations about the class turtle in the science journal. Quinton's entry was brief but accurate: "The turtle ate the worm." Quinton was well known as the most conscientious care-taker of the class pets. Tim appreciated Quinton's concern for the animals and also valued the writing and reading opportunities that came with this responsibility. Amy also recorded a message in the journal: "The worm had dirt on it." It wasn't really the written text that portrayed her dislike for worms and dirt but the way in which she read it to her friends. Everyone knew that Amy thought the class should wash the worm be-fore feeding it to the little reptile.

Two other children in the science area discovered that various things happened when they looked through the prism. Tim turned his attention to this new investigation and encouraged the children to keep track of their discoveries in the science journal. Curtis wrote, "Shape makes it look like everybody's upside-down." His idea was generative in that it

Figure 2–2

reflected a new insight for the class to explore. Throughout the day they hypothesized why that particular shape caused such a phenomenon.

Heidi noticed that Alex was carefully examining the hermit crab terrarium. She asked, "I wonder if the temperature is comfortable for the crab now? Do you think we should open or close the lid?"

Alex leaned around the side of the tank and remarked, "It's seventy-seven degrees, so you can keep it open."

The digital thermometer on the side did in fact indicate that it was a warm seventy-seven degrees, and Alex used this information to make his decision. Knowing the crab's comfort zone, Alex concluded that the class should lower the temperature by opening the lid. Of course, he was right.

In the meantime, Tray was monitoring the class graph. He posed the question this morning and documented it on large butcher paper. Building on a graph that had been constructed earlier in the year he asked, "Do you like fried eggs, scrambled eggs, or boiled eggs?"

As children were posting their preferences, Tray noticed the school principal walking down the hall. Tray motioned to Mr. Litton, "Which one do you like?" he asked confidently. Tray pointed to each option, "Fried eggs or scrambled eggs or boiled eggs?"

"Really, I don't eat eggs much at all but if I was going to eat them I guess I'd say scrambled."

"OK, then sign your name here," Tray directed as he handed him the marker.

Mr. Litton signed his name just as the other participants in this learning community did. He talked with the children about their current findings and then continued on with his business.

Daniell also began working near the graph but his intentions were different. He was measuring various features of his own body with a tape measure. He paused momentarily to write. Heidi inquired about his investigation. "I'm measuring," he responded quite matter-of-factly.

"How are you recording your ideas?" she asked.

Daniell opened his paper to show that he was illustrating each object, a strategic organizational device. We were constantly impressed by the ways in which children took charge of their learning in this environment and found creative ways to generate, record, and interpret data. Daniell's self-initiated measuring task exemplified mathematical authorship. Daniell took the initiative to pursue this investigation and then devised his own unique strategy to record the information he constructed (Figure 2–3).

FIGURE 2–3

John was working on his own mathematical investigation. He was developing an understanding of probability by recording the number of times his penny turned up heads or tails when flipping it. John had been part of a small group that had recently been exploring probability. By coloring in a chart with two columns that represented heads and tails, John was learning that each coin toss represented an independent trial and that over time heads appeared with approximately the same frequency as tails. In so doing, John was confirming and revising many of the initial hypotheses generated during the probability study group led by his teacher. Initially, many children believed that hoping for an outcome affected the toss of a coin or the roll of a die or that if a toss yielded heads then the next coin toss would be tails or that large numbers come up most often when rolling dice simply because they're bigger.

Aaron was busy building a complex structure in the block corner. Since structures in the block corner were temporary, David Whitin took a picture of it and asked Aaron to explain how he built it. Aaron began sharing his plan. He paused for a moment with that I-have-a-good-idea look in his eyes. "Why don't you take pictures from this side and then the other side?" David smiled and followed Aaron's advice, pleased that he saw the value of shifting perspectives. Architects are authors too; Aaron had created his own structure and then capitalized on the communication system of photography to represent the various perspectives that are inherent in three-dimensional constructions. As an author he was sensitive to the potential of photography to capture his design (Figure 2–4).

Aaron's appreciation for taking different perspectives was frequently evidenced in his artwork as well. His illustrations of a recent fishing trip show how he altered his stance to draw views from the top and side of the boat; he even included a fish's perspective from the water (Figure 2–5).

Heidi Mills glanced across the room and noticed two six-year-olds looking at the large inflated globe. "What do you see?" she asked.

Amy responded, "This is a big old country," pointing to the huge continent of Africa, "and this is a little bit country. And this is a big old water part."

Intrigued by Amy's current conceptions about geography, Tim joined the conversation. "Would you like to see where we live?"

"Yea, show us where Columbia, South Carolina is and where our pen pals live."

"It will be difficult to pinpoint exactly where Columbia is but we should be able to locate South Carolina," (Figure 2–6).

FIGURE 2–4

FIGURE 2–5

FIGURE 2–6

"Your pen pals live near the Mediterranean Sea in . . ."

"Italy!" both children exclaimed. They found the country shaped like a boot and began telling stories about their pen pals. The globe provided the children a context in which to discuss the relative size and shape of, as well as distance between, meaningful geographical areas.

"Let's continue this discussion later because it is time for gathering now," remarked Tim as he realized it was clean-up time.

Tim began playing the clean-up music on his guitar. Children who had been listening to taped recordings of children's books organized the listening center. Aaron and David worked on the block corner. The children who had chosen to write in their journals put them back in their cubbies and joined the group at the front of the class. Within three or four minutes everyone put their morning projects away and was seated on the floor in a semicircle at the front of the classroom.

First Gathering

Together, the children read the daily business list one item at a time. The class sang several songs beginning with "Good Morning" and concluded with a piece about feeling good. Tim turned to the children and asked, "Why do you feel good today?" Hands shot up in the air as the list evolved: "I got new glasses," "My babysitter is coming over," and "We go to the library today," were among the many reasons the children in this group were happy.

"Menu!" the children read in concert as the teacher pointed to the first item of business. The school menu was read aloud and the children responded with facial gestures that indicated their respective delight or distaste.

Next, Tim announced that it was Kenneth's turn to complete the class calendar. Kenneth decided that he should document—"We were writing in our journals"—on the calendar card since it was his turn to record an important event in school. Tim took the small rectangular sheet of colored paper off the calendar/bulletin board and recommended that Kenneth compose this idea during writing time. The class calendar functioned as a group learning log. The children took turns recording insights about the classroom as well as significant personal experiences. Although calendars are typically considered mathematical texts, the lines between mathematics and language become blurred during strategies such as this one where both were so richly contextualized (Figure 2–7).

"Stick calendar" was the next item of business. As soon as Tim mentioned this task Sheree cried out in delight, "Yea!"

Tim continued, "Today is," he paused motioning for the children's assistance. "Thursday, January 31, 1989. Today is number *31*."

FIGURE 2–7

"We bundled the tens together yesterday," remarked Sheree. "You need one more."

"Thank you," was the teacher's reply as he placed a popsicle stick in the one's bag. This daily task highlighted the functionality of the regrouping strategy. Tim turned the discussion over to the children. He believed it was crucial for them to learn to ask good questions while functioning as teachers and learners. Which day of the month is the nearest the middle? How many days since my birthday? How many Sundays in this month? How many school days were there in this month? Because the discussions were open and the children played an active role in the experience, they often used this project to make personal connections between the days, weeks, and months of the year on the class calendar. We also found that the ones and tens bags assisted the children in understanding place value. Addition and subtraction that required regrouping could naturally be connected to the place value activity completed for every day of the month.

Personal surveys were next on the agenda. Each day during morning choice time, three children were encouraged to conduct personal surveys on a topic of their choice. They collected, organized, and shared their data in their own ways. Daniell's work was featured today. Because Dave was working closely with Daniell, Tim invited them both to share.

Dave explained that Daniell took the measuring tape and ruler from the math shelf and began measuring different things. Using Daniell's text he described the process that Daniell went through as he composed his measurement survey.

"He started by drawing a picture of the measuring tape on the top of the paper. Then I helped him find the distance around his head and he wrote "54." I asked him how he would remember it was his head." Daniell showed the class how he solved this problem by pointing to his picture and naming all of the body parts including his ribs. He had obviously drawn upon the knowledge he had gained during a recent study of the human body. He used numerals to record specific measurements. "Ohhheee!" was the audience's enthusiastic response.

"You made a good nine," concluded one of Daniell's good friends.

Delighted that Daniell extended a measuring experience from last week, Tim made connections between Daniell's current project and the previous week's lesson where the children worked in pairs to measure and record observations about a series of objects. He emphasized how pleased he was that Daniell went beyond what they had done together to create his own survey.

Next, Tray was invited to explain his class graph. Tray emphasized the word *or* as he read his question. "Do you like fried eggs or scrambled eggs or boiled eggs?"

David asked, "Tray, why did you put *or* between each choice?"

"Because you can only choose one," Tray responded rather matter-of-factly, demonstrating the logic in his planning. If he hadn't incorporated *or* into his question, the children may have selected more than one. With the use of this two-letter word, Tray efficiently made the conditions of this question clear. One choice was needed to fairly determine the class favorite. Tray was an author who was sensitive to the mathematical language that he was using.

"Who would like to say something about this graph?" Tray asked. It was customary for the child who was sharing to call on participants and so the children and adults in the room raised their hands to share observations and insights.

Lena was the first to raise her hand. "More people signed up right here," she said pointing to the fried eggs. She counted the list of names and then read, "Fried eggs."

Alex referred to the last column and said, "Two people here." As he attempted to read the last option his friends could tell he was stuck.

"It begins with *B* . . ." and "Boiled," several of his classmates read together.

"This many people have the most," remarked Quinton as he pointed to the fried eggs.

Curtis extended Quinton's observation by remarking, "Boiled eggs and scrambled eggs are the least."

Tim also participated by sharing his thoughts about the topic. "When I saw what Tray was doing I predicted in my mind which one would have the most and the least. I wasn't sure which one would have the most but I was pretty sure that boiled eggs would have the least. And I was right. Only two people chose boiled eggs so I can see that my prediction was correct." By waiting to be called on and participating in the observations along with the children, Tim demonstrated the value of predicting and that he was a learner as well. He too had to wait to be called on and his ideas were not privileged over the children's in this learning community.

Michael asked and answered his own question, "What if you took these two off boiled eggs? Then we would only have seventeen."

Next, Heidi acknowledged Tray's concern for gathering accurate information when his friend wanted to revise his vote. She commented, "Curtis realized he signed up under fried eggs and he doesn't like fried eggs. Tray let him change his mind."

And so the conversation continued.

When it was Sheree's turn to share her survey she carefully made her way through the group to the front of the class so as not to step on anyone's fingers. "Sheree has something important to share," remarked Tim as he introduced her topic to the group. Sheree asked if anyone could read her survey question.

"Mr. O'Keefe," said Sheree in a shy yet confident way. He had raised his hand too.

"I think I know because we have been doing surveys like this," remarked the teacher featuring the importance of making predictions based on what would make sense in this particular context. "How many people are here?"

"Yea!" Sheree exclaimed as her smile widened.

Careful examination of the question and her responses indicated that there were fourteen children present when she conducted her personal attendance survey. Sheree had divided her paper into sections with a series of horizontal and vertical lines. In this way she was planning space for many days to come.

"I'm gonna do it each day!" Sheree noted demonstrating her interest in tracking this data over time, as she concluded her sharing session. Sheree's interest in this project grew out of the class's prolonged engagements in recording the daily attendance and the group's current fascination with attendance graphs. Together, they were uncovering various ways to collect, organize, and display attendance information. They shared their texts with each other and used alternative forms of communication while analyzing and revising their strategies to communicate their meaning most effectively.

Curtis was next. He created his own graph this morning. It represented an interest in loose and growing teeth that was common to this group of six year olds. While Curtis' questions were original, they demonstrated the generative nature of authoring as they built upon a graph the teacher had constructed earlier in the week.

"How many teeth have you grown?" Curtis read as he shared his first question with his colleagues. As he began to discuss his findings, he raised an important matter. Curtis informed the group that some of his respondents simply wrote their names; this strategy was often appropriate for class graphs but not for this one. "But I want them to write the number of it too," Curtis explained, acknowledging that some of the children did document the number of new teeth they had grown via numerals or number words.

Tim made connections between the strategies needed to complete this task and an earlier experience. "This is sort of like a follow-up survey to the one we did earlier this week. I originally asked, 'How many teeth have you lost?' Curtis asked, 'How many teeth have you grown?' He expanded the idea a bit" (Figure 2–8).

Aaron felt the spaces in his teeth with his tongue and then remarked, "I lost two teeth."

Aaron's comment triggered another issue for Curtis. Pointing to the right side of the paper he read, "How many teeth have you lost?" He continued, "I wanted some people to sign over here and over here," pointing to both columns.

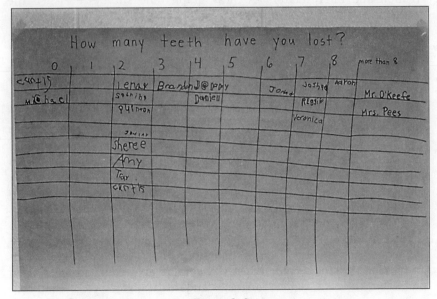

FIGURE 2–8

David responded by asking, "What could you do next time to be sure people do that?"

"I could make some boxes."

"You might even put numbers at the top and if they lost two then they could sign there; or if they lost three they could sign up under number three and so on," David said, referring to the teeth graph Tim made with the class.

"Then they won't have to write the numbers!" was Curtis' enthusiastic response to this revision suggestion. He realized an alternative format would provide a more detailed and accurate picture of his data and would enable him to interpret it more efficiently.

Tray had another idea. "Why didn't Curtis write numbers on the bottom and have people circle the number for the teeth they lost with their name?" He extended his recommendation with the suggestion that Curtis use a class roster to keep track of who had responded. Referring back to his egg graph he noted, "I put a *zero* for Brandon so I would remember he hadn't voted."

As the class continued to explore the communication and learning potential of graphing they were thinking like authors who valued the process of revision in mathematics; they recognized the importance of working together to solve problems and the value of generating several alternatives to most effectively display numerical information. Children were using the language of mathematics in the rich context of their own creations and those of their peers. Each person who contributed to the creation and interpretation of these graphs and surveys enriched the mathematical conversation.

Writing Time

The class was dismissed after determining whose turn it was to share journals. Generally, three children per day shared journals; this was determined alphabetically. However, additional children were given the opportunity to share if they created something special or completed a publication. They simply added their names to the list on the board.

Some children went directly to their cubbies to gather their journals and favorite writing utensils. Others joined Mrs. Pees at the table that had become a message writing spot during uninterrupted writing time. They began writing messages to one another and posting them on the message board. A couple of children decided that they wanted to have written conversations with the adults in the room. As they constructed their meanings across various writing contexts they demonstrated how fluid the lines between communication systems become when children are allowed to access them in their own ways. Art, written language, and mathematics were used in concert, each complementing and extending the message portrayed by the others. They also showed us what happens when children are respected as authors and encouraged to write about what they know and care about.

Three children used mathematics in their writing this morning. Alex rehearsed his memory of number words by writing them in linear fashion (Figure 2–9). Like most children who make lists such as this, Alex began with *one*. He moved down the page writing two, three, four, five, and six quite conventionally. After finding that he was out of space, he revised his strategy by moving to the top of the page to complete his list. He finished this self-initiated piece quickly and so began working on another list of words he had committed to memory. Tim had been tracking Alex's writing growth. He appreciated Alex's attention to conventional spelling but was concerned about the fact that he seemed to value writing what he could spell over writing for genuine communication or learning. Consequently, Tim asked Alex if he would be interested in a written conversation. Alex responded by telling his teacher that he wanted him to ask the questions. Following Alex's lead, the teacher posed questions that would allow Alex to write familiar words in a meaningful way (Figure 2–10).

Tim asked, "How old are you?" highlighting the functional nature of numbers.

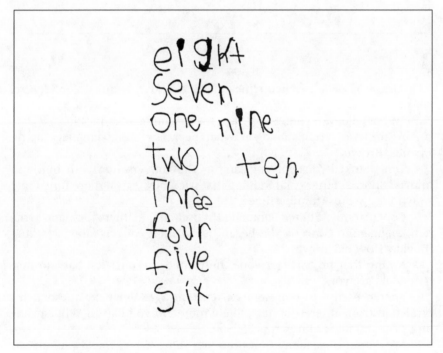

FIGURE 2–9

FIGURE 2–10

Alex was delighted with the question and responded confidently, "Six."

"What color are your eyes?" was the teacher's next question.

Again, Alex could build on what he knew about language as he wrote, "Brown."

Tim thanked Alex for engaging in the conversation with him and moved on to another child, hoping that Alex now saw a more functional way to use words from his repertoire.

Concurrently, Sheree competently used art, mathematics, and written language in concert. She began her written conversation by asking David, "How old are you?"

Noting that he was forty-one, he turned the question back to her. "How old are you?"

Sheree used *6* to represent her current age. Her next question revealed a strong interest of hers. She wrote, "Do you like JB WB," meaning, "Do you like to jump rope?"

"Yes, I do. How many times can you jump?" was David's inquiry as he was aware of the fact that the children in this class were graphing their own rope jumping accomplishments and continually setting new challenges for themselves.

"Ninety," was Sheree's impressive answer.

"Who plays jump rope with you?"

"Mr. O'Keefe," she replied (Figure 2–11).

The conversation continued. Both participants used art, mathematics, and language to learn more about each other. The opportunity to access alternative communication systems to reflect and extend

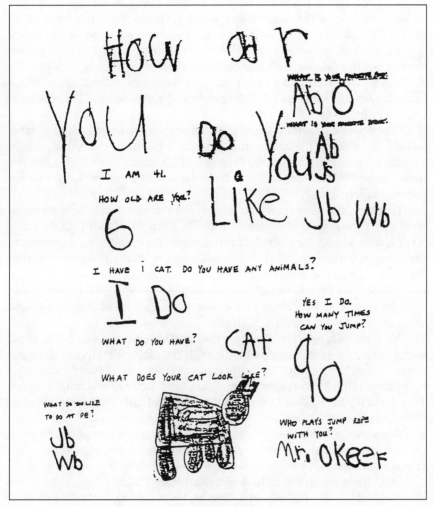

FIGURE 2–11

meaning was critical to these texts. The experience of conversing on paper also encouraged authors to write about what they know and to pose their own questions.

Second Gathering

Tim began playing an instrumental tune on his guitar to indicate that it was time to clean up and join him at the front of the class. Children who had been working with Mrs. Pees posted their messages on the message board. Kenneth returned the markers he had been using to illustrate his calendar card and the others put their journals in their cubbies. Tim reminded the children who wrote their names on the sharing list to place their journals on the chalkboard ledge. He asked the group to scoot back a bit so he could plug the microphone into the record player. They used a microphone during sharing time so that the audience could hear soft voices clearly.

Tim invited Kenneth to read the calendar entry. Although he spoke in a whisper, his message could be heard and appreciated. "We was writing in our journals."

"Good work Kenneth. I really like how you put lots of detail in your picture. You drew the table and the pencil holders—everything," said Tim as he recognized a critical feature of Kenneth's text. The teacher took Kenneth's calendar card and tacked it on the appropriate square on the class calendar.

Together, the class reviewed the days of the week and the number of weeks in January. In the midst of a rich discussion about dates, days, weeks, and years, they also reflected upon the important experiences that were recorded in this class journal. After several children noted that January 31 was the last day of the month, Tim said he would take the cards down after school so they could bind them on Friday. Each monthly calendar was made into a class book that contained events and ideas unique to this group of learners.

Alex and Reggie read their journal entries to the class. Next, Heidi asked Tray to help her share a riddle with the class. She invited Tray because he was the first one to figure it out that morning. Tray held out his hand displaying three coins: one nickel, one penny, and one quarter. Tray recited the riddle, "Johnny's mother had three children, Penny, Nicole, and . . . ?"

There was a hush in the room as the children attempted to complete the sentence. Hands began to rise. When Tray called on Quinton, he guessed "Penny."

"No," Tray remarked as he selected another child.

"D . . . d . . . d . . . dime—ah—Donna," was Sabrina's prediction.

"Tray, tell it again, and *you* listen very carefully," Heidi responded, directing her final comment to the class.

Tray recited the riddle once again. Several children named Penny and Nicole. "Kids who said *Penny* and *Nicole* are right because they are both her children, but now we have to think of the third child." "One more time Tray," said Tim.

As Tray spoke, his teacher took dictation on the board. The children watched intently as the oral language was transcribed. "Johnny!" exclaimed Alex as he pointed to the first word of the sentence. The written form of the text provided children the opportunity to inspect the message much more carefully. In addition, the children redirected their attention away from the coins, which were intended to trick them. That reflection led to the answer.

"Alex got it," responded Tim as he underlined Johnny's name. Tray grinned from ear to ear and resumed his position in the group.

Heidi initiated a brief strategy-sharing session as she reflected on her original prediction. "You know when I heard this the first time I thought it might be George because I was looking at the picture on the quarter. George Washington's picture was on the quarter."

"Hey, that picture of Washington looks like John," cried Tray as he made a connection between the riddle's answer and Heidi's original strategy.

Tim responded by slowly rereading the written version on the board and then asked for other problem-solving ideas. Some children said they could only think of the names in the story. Dave validated Sabrina's idea by describing how she tried to think of a word that sounded like *dime* since *Nicole* was similar to *Nickel*: "*Dime, Donna* like *Nicole* and *Nickel*."

Uncovering Mathematics Through Children's Literature

David read to the class one of his favorite folktales entitled *Two Ways to Count to Ten* by Ruby Dee (1988). In this story a contest is held to determine who is to succeed tiger as king of the jungle. The successor is to be that animal who successfully hurls the mighty tiger's javelin into the sky and counts to ten before the javelin hits the ground. All the animals fail, including the mighty lion, until the clever antelope throws the javelin skyward and reaches ten quickly by counting by twos. A discussion about the tricky main character naturally evolved as he concluded the story. David responded to the group's questions and insights and then redirected their attention to a follow-up experience—"Remember the photos of Veronica counting by twos?"—referring to the counting strategy that Veronica used to show even numbers. "She held up the pointer on each hand and said, 'Two.' Then she added the middle finger to each hand and said, 'Four,' continuing to add fingers until she reached ten."

"Several weeks ago people were cutting out pictures of one, two, three, four, and five fingers. We were trying to find out names for each of these numbers by cutting out different combinations of fingers. But when we got to six do you know what we had to do?"

"Three plus three," was the initial response.

"Yes, and someone did something else too. Aaron what did you do?"

"Five plus one."

"He found a five and a one and then glued them on the paper." After discussing other possible number combinations for six, David invited the children to create names for larger numbers.

"Mrs. Pees, hold up the number at your table." Mrs. Pees held up the number card at her table. "If you like the number 9 [referring to the number on Mrs. Pees's card], you may want to choose the nine table. There are tables with seven, eight, nine and ten. Here's your challenge. As a group, see if you can cut out fingers to make the number at your table. Use as many combinations as possible."

The children made their choices and settled in for a productive group project. Several children began cutting out various finger combinations. The adults recommended that the children might begin by thinking about a familiar combination that equaled a certain number. Tim demonstrated this notion when he asked, "Reggie, can you think of some ways to make ten already?"

Reggie kept cutting intently and remarked, "Five and five."

"OK, five plus five is a good way to make ten. Quinton, can you think of another way to make ten?"

Quinton nodded without responding, not ready for an interruption. Aaron chimed in, "Change seven and three to five and two and three."

"So, you can use three pictures; a *five* plus a *two* and a *three* to make ten. That's a good idea!" The teacher emphasized the significance of Aaron's discovery so that other children might follow his lead (Figure 2–12).

Then he returned to Quinton. He noticed that Quinton had a *five* and a *one* so far. "Quinton, count all of the fingers you have so far."

"One, two, three, four, five, six."

"So how many more do you need to make ten?" Quinton looked up at his teacher, smiled and then selected a hand with four fingers up. "Excellent Quinton."

David was working with another small group. Sabrina created a five and four combination and then composed the mathematical text using numerals: $5 + 4 = 9$ (Figure 2–13).

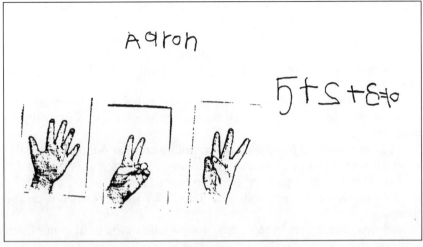

FIGURE 2–12

"How do you know that's nine?" David asked.

She held up her fingers and wiggled each one as she counted to nine. "Can you figure out another way to show it's nine without counting each one?"

Sabrina was puzzled at that request and so David revised his

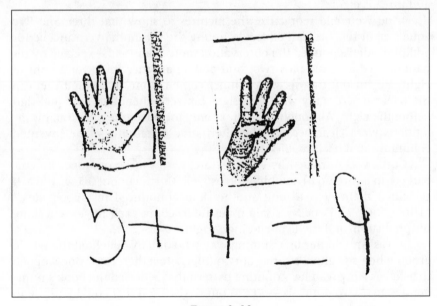

FIGURE 2–13

challenge to provide support. "How much is this?" David asked holding up both hands with fingers open wide.

"Ten," she said immediately.

"What happens if we lower one finger?"

Sabrina lowered one of her fingers and commented with a proud smile, "Nine."

"Good, that's another way to figure it out. If five and five equals ten, then five plus four is nine." They both acted the scenario out again on their fingers.

"I know four and four," she said recalling another doubles fact (facts in which both addends are the same number).

"Good, what must you add to get to nine?"

Sabrina raised a finger and said, "One." She then recorded it on the group's paper.

Sabrina, like others in this class, used doubles facts to help her learn other combinations. She also demonstrated the effectiveness of fingers as a tool for understanding numerical relationships. The strategy of building off the familiar doubles facts became clear through this engagement.

The exploration at Heidi's table was also revealing. Amy, John, Alex, and Curtis were working together to devise as many combinations as possible to make eight.

Heidi asked, "Did you hear what Curtis said?" directing the group's attention to a new insight. Curtis shared his latest combination, "Five and three is eight."

"And we could reorganize the pictures to show that three and five equals eight too," remarked Heidi, noting the commutative principle for addition. Alex extended the observation more than Heidi expected by renaming five as three plus two, and adding another three for a sum of eight. He cut out the necessary finger combinations and glued them to the paper horizontally with plus signs between them and an equal sign before the eight. Although Alex's text only included one numeral, his intentions were clear because the alternative equation that he invented communicated his idea effectively.

Curtis was intrigued by Alex's strategy. Not to be outdone, he embarked on a three-part combination as well. Curtis cut out a *3*, *4*, and a *1*. He glued them next to one another and announced his "good idea." "Three, four, and one," he said, pausing to count each finger, checking his prediction, and then concluding, "Eight."

It was Amy in her unassuming way who quietly delighted the whole group when she glued a series of two fingers together. Everyone stopped to listen as Amy read her counting pattern that reflected the book's number design. "Two, four, six—oh I'm out of twos." "What could you use to make two?" asked Heidi. Although Amy was quite capable of solving this problem herself, the children were so accustomed to supporting each other that she turned to her friends for help.

"Here, you can have two of my ones," exclaimed Curtis feeling proud about being so helpful.

"Thanks," replied Amy as she glued them on the paper. Just then another child found a two-finger combination and so donated it to Amy's cause. Amy grinned and placed it below the two individual fingers (Figure 2–14).

In response to this challenge, the children taught each other and the adults in the room. As authors of mathematical ideas, they tested hypotheses and made predictions; they checked their predictions by confirming some and revising others and continued to work together toward a common goal. As they did they stopped to reflect and recognize

FIGURE 2–14

each other's contributions. As authors they capitalized on their background knowledge of using fingers to solve mathematical problems; they used this strategy to make further insights into mathematical patterns and relationships. Finally, they were authors who grew together as they stretched each other's thinking by creating a variety of names for different numbers. They were using the most familiar manipulative of fingers to better understand the important mathematical concept of equivalence.

Uninterrupted Reading Time

As the groups created their final combinations, Tim announced that they could line up for recess. The children and adults played together outside and talked about the significance of the morning's activities. After about fifteen minutes, the teacher gathered the group together again and reminded them to begin thinking about a book they would like to read during quiet reading time. Once they returned to the room, all participants found a good book and comfortable location to read. Some chose to read a big book together, a couple of children selected class-made books, while the others picked texts from the children's book collection housed on the bookshelves. A soft hum spread throughout the room as everyone settled in to their reading. The hum continued until Tray reminded Tim that it was almost lunch time. Getting to lunch on time was a powerful reason for learning to read the classroom clock! With Tray's announcement, the children returned the books and began washing their hands in preparation for lunch.

The rest of the day unfolded much like the morning. The teacher, children, tutor, and researchers continued to shape and reshape this powerful learning environment together.

Reflections

To truly appreciate the learning potential of the curriculum, it is helpful to tease out the concepts and strategies children learned as they engaged in mathematical authorship. The learning experiences were so naturally embedded within the curricular framework, significant incidents could easily be overlooked. To illustrate the ways in which the children were learning to think like mathematicians, we have identified key features of the curriculum that promoted mathematical literacy. We have also highlighted the strategies children used to develop an understanding of several important mathematical concepts. When perusing Table 2–1, please imagine the days that preceded and followed this particular one to develop a vision of the ways in which Tim's children developed mathematical literacy.

Table 2–1   Reflecting on the Day's Events

Demonstrations of Authorship	Classroom Context	Mathematical Concept	Strategies for Understanding
Authors grow through prolonged engagements.	Sign-in journal	Quantity	Counting, comparing, making predictions
Authors use alternative communication systems to reflect and extend meaning.	A board game constructed by children	Equivalence	Counting on to find sum
Authors share their observations with others.	The hermit crab terrarium	Temperature	Counting
Authors share their texts with others.	A class graph on eggs	Quantity	Comparing, classifying
Authors use alternative communication systems to reflect and extend meaning.	Measuring equipment available on the mathematics shelf	Length	Measuring
Authors grow through prolonged engagements.	Classroom game of penny toss	Probability	Counting, noting patterns
Authors initiate their own investigations.	Building in the block corner	Spatial relations	Comparing
Authors share their observations with others.	Examining a classroom inflated globe	Area	Comparing
Authors write about what they know.	The class calendar	Time	Measuring
Authors grow through prolonged engagements.	The stick calendar	Place value (base)	Counting, classifying
Authors initiate their own investigations.	Personal survey on attendance	Quantity	Counting
Authors revise their texts; authors reflect on past demonstrations and generate new texts.	Personal survey on teeth	Quantity	Classifying, comparing
Authors write about what they know.	Written conversation during journal time	Time	Measuring

Table 2–1 continued

Demonstrations of Authorship	Classroom Context	Mathematical Concept	Strategies for Understanding
Authors use alternative communication systems to reflect and extend meaning.	The sharing of *Two Ways to Count to Ten*	Quantity, equivalence	Simplifying a problem, noting patterns

The Investigations of One Author: Aaron

Aaron in the block corner

While we see that it is important to study several children's reactions to single projects, we also feel that observing one child across several mathematical literacy events opens new insights and opportunities for us to learn from our students. This kind of observation serves as a cross reference. Watching how an individual changes, develops, and grows in mathematics gives us yet another perspective on how communication through mathematics develops among all children. Jerry Harste points out the value of case studies in studying language development. Since we are looking at mathematics from a whole language perspective, we believe that this also holds true when considering the development of mathematical literacy. Harste notes that generalized stage models don't necessarily hold true for individuals yet there may be one person who occasionally can demonstrate more fully the potential of a learning community (Harste 1989). All data collected is not equally informative. Aaron, however, because of his willingness to share his thoughts and insights, really helped us to understand some of the processes that young children go through when exploring mathematics. After seeing from the beginning of the year Aaron's willingness to share his questions, observations, and in-process thoughts, Tim O'Keefe paid particular attention to Aaron at work and play.

We have chosen Aaron to be the focus of this chapter. In many respects he is not unlike the other children in this transition first-grade class. Aaron's score on the readiness test in the fall fell below the score designated as being ready for first grade. By this standardized measurement, he was a child of below average ability, and would probably need an extra year of first grade before going on to second. It is important to note that we feel the screening test taken by the students is, at best, a gross predictor of student success. For some, it did reflect the need for an extra year of first grade. For other children, the test was not a useful tool in this prediction. One child in Aaron's class, for example, tested the highest of any first grader in the school on the statewide test in the spring with a perfect score. In Aaron's case, this year proved to be an important transition. He was allowed the extra time he needed to develop academic and social skills, and was encouraged to show his creativity through art, language, and mathematical communication.

Aaron was naturally quiet and unassuming. His slender build and subdued manner were only a facade for his active curiosity and insightfulness. At times, Aaron became a class leader inspiring others with his questions. At other times he followed the lead of his peers and learned from their queries. This curiosity and his willingness to demonstrate his ideas to the class proved to be a real asset. With encouragement, Aaron chose to look at situations analytically, much like a mathematician. His interest in measurement and data collection proved contagious. Much of Aaron's strength in mathematics would be difficult to measure on a standardized test or through worksheets where only single right answers are acceptable. Aaron could perform the usual array of pencil-and-paper tasks, albeit not fast enough to be considered at "mastery" level for the district-mandated timed math-facts tests. Aaron's real strength lay in his ability to think about situations and events mathematically. He used numbers and attributes to describe, to measure, to record, and to communicate. He asked and answered questions that intrigued him. His use of mathematics went far beyond the classroom at math time. Aaron naturally used mathematics to extend his personal interests as well as class themes. We found that making some of his insights public by sharing them at class meetings motivated others to look at things analytically and gave Aaron the opportunity to view his work from a different perspective. Once he saw that his explorations were interesting to his teacher and peers, he sought out new patterns and ways to use mathematics to continue to educate himself and the class.

The Halloween Survey

From the beginning of the year it was clear that Aaron enjoyed collecting and organizing data in various ways. Sometimes the process of collecting data seemed very important to him. He enjoyed the social act of asking questions and recording answers. At other times the data was secondary to his interest in the systematic ordering of information. Aaron would spend a lot of time reformatting his data in ways that were easier to understand. One way Aaron and others in the class gathered data was by conducting class surveys. At the beginning of the year this experience was simply called "walking around the room."

A few days before Halloween, Aaron came to school, eagerly signed in, put his belongings in his cubby, and searched for an empty clipboard, anxious to initiate a personal survey. Seeing this energy, Aaron's teacher, Tim, asked about his current project. "I'm going to ask what kids like about Halloween," Aaron said, barely looking up from his paper. Aaron started construction of his survey by taking a ruler and neatly drawing a straight line across the top of his sheet. Abandoning the ruler for expediency, he drew a rectangle roughly divided into ten spaces. Confident in his ability to represent ideas through art, Aaron began drawing pictures to represent this holiday theme. He drew a witch flying on a broom in the top left section of his paper. He wrote the word *black* above his creation. "That's so they'll know what color she's supposed to be." Next to the witch, Aaron drew a "scary mask" complete with a sutured forehead, and then a jack-o'-lantern. In his second row Aaron illustrated a ghost, a bat (again he wrote the word *black* to make the color of the creature clear), and another ghost with the word *white* inscribed above. In the last row Aaron cleverly depicted a haunted house complete with ornate shutters and a fence.

Aaron walked around the room gathering responses to "Which ones do you like?" from eleven of his peers. Aaron chose to record responses by writing each respondent's first initial, with the exception of Amy, whom he recorded as *AH*. Later he told us that he used this strategy to avoid confusion among the three children in the class whose names started with *A*: Amy, Alex, and Aaron himself. Thus Aaron was adapting his data collection strategy slightly to fit this situation. Reggie recorded his own choice by writing his entire name in the space for black bat (Figure 3–1).

FIGURE 3–1

Aaron used sophisticated organizational skills in his data gathering. He provided the class with seven options and allowed more than one choice per person. His decision to record initials rather than entire names was strategic because he did not have enough space to record the full names.

In creating and sharing his Halloween survey with the class Aaron proved himself to be an author of mathematical ideas. Since this and other surveys completed by Aaron were his ideas and the means for generating and recording information were unique, he clearly constructed and owned the text. Aaron enjoyed Halloween and his text included symbols that he knew represented the holiday. His use of alternate communication systems in the creation of his survey also gives credence to his authoring status.

What Are You Going to Be When You Grow Up?

Aaron conducted a similar survey on a different topic in February. His interest this time—"What Are You Going to Be When You Grow Up?"— was ingeniously displayed in a form similar to his Halloween survey. Aaron allowed the children in the class to choose more than one occupation. This opportunity to make several choices demonstrated the idea that people can do more than one thing as a grown-up. For example, a teacher could also be a writer, as Amy expressed in her choices.

In designing this instrument, Aaron started out with a set of options but he added other choices during his interviewing and made drawings of other careers suggested by his classmates. He modified his instrument as he collected more data. Thus, he displayed another characteristic of authors of mathematical ideas by reflecting on and revising his text. His flexibility in changing the instrument showed his concern for recording authentic data. We saw this as a real sign of growth for Aaron. Instead of trying to force responses to fit his ideas of what kids should do as grownups, he was open to including those of his peers.

By its completion, Aaron's survey contained twenty-eight different occupations. In his words they were (left to right and top to bottom): making garages, making houses, entering fishing tournaments and winning money and trophies, being a truck driver, being a doctor, building motorcycles, being a police officer, being an artist, being a nurse, driving an ambulance, being a fireman, driving a boat, being a sheriff's man, making surfboards, making boats, being a teacher, being a writer, making skis, making ski rope, being a clown, making toys, making masks, taking care of lakes ("Setting a stick to see how high the water is going to get"), making camper sales, making kites, being a dog catcher, and making stop signs. The diversity of these choices demonstrates the confidence that Aaron displayed as an author who was willing to represent a variety of career options for his classmates.

In conducting this questionnaire, Aaron had some research associates. When Brandon decided that he wanted to be a truck driver, his curiosity was also piqued. Brandon decided to design a similar survey with different choices. Unashamed about adapting Aaron's idea, he created another instrument for assessing vocational aspirations.

Michael also became interested in the project. With Aaron's permission, he picked up his own clipboard and shadowed Aaron, recording the initials of those interviewed. In this way the team could keep better track of who had been asked since Michael's paper had only initials whereas Aaron's pages were filled with additional information. Michael's checklist was used to be sure that each person in class was asked only once. Michael's effort was complementary to Aaron's, who could focus more on his questioning and data formatting.

Aaron and Michael took two days to complete the survey to their satisfaction. Seventeen children and two teachers were asked to respond, leaving out of the survey only one child, who was absent for these two days.

By designing and following through with his questionnaire, Aaron demonstrated characteristics we feel represent an author of mathematical ideas. Aaron wrote about what he knew; he included many of his favorite activities and pastimes in his survey as well as those of his parents, friends, and acquaintances. Aaron shared his mathematical text with others during his data collection and also at a class meeting. This recognition was important to Aaron and his classmates and by making his ideas public others benefited from the methodology used in this survey. He confidently used the alternate communication systems of art and oral and written language to convey ideas and record information. While we can't say for sure what was going through Aaron's mind during the creation of his survey, it certainly appears that writing down ideas for jobs generated other ideas. Building garages was followed by building houses, making skis was followed by making ski ropes, being a teacher was followed by being a writer. Thus, Aaron nicely demonstrated the generative nature of authoring. Aaron and Michael carefully asked every child and adult in the class to respond. This example, as well as other projects that Aaron initiated, demonstrates Aaron's prolonged engagement with a mathematical task. Aaron had complete ownership of his text throughout the process. While students and teachers assisted with questions and offered alternative choices not already present in his survey, this investigation belonged to Aaron. Aaron felt strongly that he was a member of the mathematical "literacy club" (Smith 1988). As stated earlier, Aaron revised his text to accommodate unexpected responses from the children he surveyed. This single experience does a nice job of spotlighting Aaron as a mathematical author with originality in content and form.

What Do You Like: Lima Beans or String Beans?

Aaron was quick to capitalize on class themes, as he did in his survey about beans. In the spring during a unit on plant life, Aaron brought to school many vegetable seeds from home. Since his family plants a garden each year, our unit conveniently dovetailed with his family's project. After showing his seeds to the class and telling which kinds of plants grow from them, David Whitin suggested that Aaron might want to do a survey using his seeds. Aaron accepted the invitation by choosing two that he knew, a lima bean seed and a string bean seed. After gathering the tools he would need to conduct his survey, Aaron held the seeds beside his paper and carefully drew each one with a pen. Not being completely satisfied with the pen drawings, Aaron revised his text by coloring a picture of each seed above his pen drawings. To try to get as close to the actual colors as possible, Aaron used two different coloring instruments. For the lima bean he chose a dark, rust-colored marker, and for the string bean he chose a brown crayon, carefully leaving an oval-shaped white spot in the center. Aaron then asked a question—"What do you like: lima beans or string beans?"—of fifteen people in the room, recording their responses himself under the proper columns. Aaron recorded mostly initials for efficiency with two exceptions: Brandon became *Br* and Mr. O'Keefe became *Mr.* (Figure 3–2).

To conclude his project Aaron recorded two observations that focused on the inequality of his findings. "The lima beans is having not a lot," and "string beans got the most." Children need opportunities to discuss mathematical concepts in different ways. Aaron capitalized on this chance to say which choice had more and less in his own way. In the short time that it took for Aaron to complete and share his survey, he learned and taught the class many things. He demonstrated a systematic and effective way of gathering, organizing, and presenting data using art and written language. He also showed that, like other surveys, the sets of data aren't completely separate. One person, Joshua, selected both types of beans and Aaron accommodated him by placing his initials under both columns. This is not unlike other kinds of surveys or opinion polls where a person's response may well fit under more than one category.

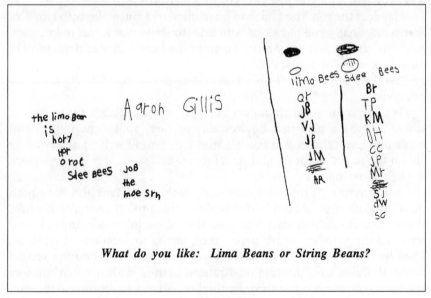

What do you like: Lima Beans or String Beans?

FIGURE 3–2

Aaron arranged the initials of his respondents in such a way that one glance at his data indicated the class preference. This nearly one-to-one placement of initials was strategic in that it gave easy access to the conclusions Aaron drew from his data.

Without using a single numeral, Aaron created an interesting and worthwhile mathematical text. His planful collection and insightful observations of his data show how a young mathematical author can work in an environment that allows for creativity and exploration. Aaron enjoyed using graphs and surveys to explore via mathematics topics that interested him. Through sharing his methods and results with the class, everyone became aware of the power of this kind of data collection and its potential for organizing and displaying data.

Exploring Mathematics at Home

Aaron showed that his interest in mathematics went well beyond surveys. About two weeks later, he created a very different kind of mathematical text at home in which he practiced some basic addition facts. Aaron came to school one morning and handed his teacher a paper with sixty addition equations written in his own hand and answered correctly. "Mr. O'Keefe, I did some homework," was all he said as he handed over his work.

"Wow, Aaron!" Tim said, particularly pleased since no homework was assigned. "Did you just give yourself all of these problems?"

"Look at the top," he said, and he pointed to a single die with two dots drawn diagonally and marks on both sides to show that it was rolling.

"I'm very impressed, Aaron. So you rolled some dice and made all of these problems for yourself?"

"No," he answered, "I only had one dice so I rolled it two times for each one."

We knew how much Aaron enjoyed playing games using dice at school and were glad that he was able to carry that same enthusiasm home and use it there. Tim asked Aaron if he would write down what he did on the paper so they could remember it and share it with the class at the next meeting.

Aaron wrote, "I rolled the dice and set the plus signs and the equals signs" (Figure 3–3). Aaron had worked at this project for quite a while. When demonstrating his project to the class, he rolled the die and recorded the number on his paper, recognizing the amount at a glance. Then he rolled the die again and recorded the plus sign and the second numeral. Using the counting-on strategy(starting with the first number and then counting on by ones), he used his fingers to determine the sum and wrote the equal sign and the answer.

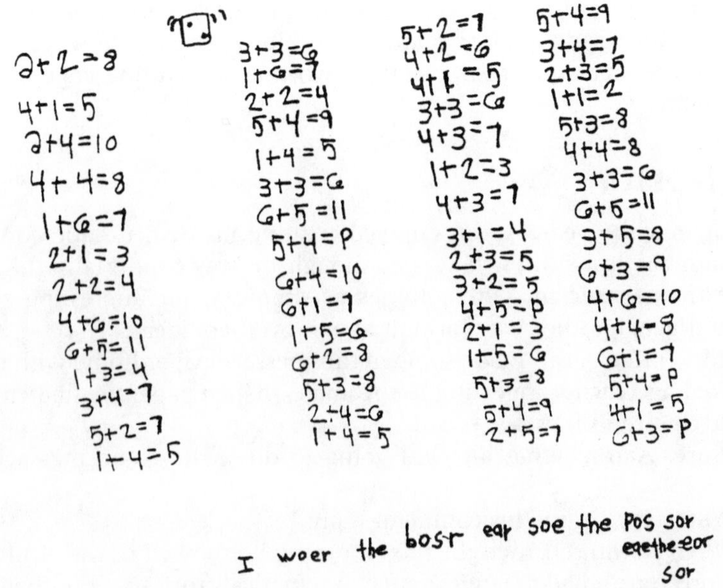

Aaron's self-initiated homework project.

FIGURE 3–3

This mathematical text appears quite different from Aaron's surveys. While his dice game text consisted entirely of numerals and mathematical symbols, his surveys were devoid of such signs. However, Aaron still demonstrates features of authorship. He built on his interest in games. He felt strongly about sharing his work with his teacher and made it public by describing his activity at a class meeting. He constructed and owned the text. It was his idea and he showed pride in his completed product. While Aaron's revisions may not be apparent at first glance, note that the first two sixes in his text are backwards. Perhaps at some point he decided that they did not look right and from that point on whenever he wrote a six he formed it conventionally. At this time Aaron still had not decided about the direction of nines but given his apparent need to have things done properly, we were confident that with more experience he would revise the appearance of these numerals as well.

In this activity Aaron confirmed an observation that we had been noting for a long time: many children seem to know exactly what they need to work on, and when provided with opportunities they will often work on those areas that need strengthening. It is only when children are given support to explore mathematical ideas and create ways to represent these ideas that they can truly work at the cutting edge of their own ability.

Apple Math

Throughout the year, Aaron enjoyed creating his own unique contexts for mathematical stories. It was as though he was continually thinking like a mathematician. Often, things as simple as an interesting shape would trigger another way for him to express these ideas.

"Mr. O'Keefe, can I take some of this message paper home with me?" he asked his teacher, referring to the apple-shaped paper we had cut out for the children's message board.

"Sure, Aaron, what are you going to do, write some messages at home?"

"You'll see," came his confident reply.

When Aaron returned the next morning he showed us the "fruits" of his effort. Aaron had created some mathematical stories on the theme of apples (Figure 3–4).

When asked to share what his three stories meant Aaron said, "Two apples fell off the tree. One was rotten. So there was one left." (In his first equation, Aaron revised the operation from addition to subtraction but had not completely erased the addition sign.) Aaron had cleverly colored his rotten apple brown and the healthy apple red. On the other side of his apple tree, he created another subtraction problem with the same format. "Four apples fell off the tree. One was rotten, so there was three." Stapled to his first two subtraction scenarios was another apple story. "There was four apples and three was rotten so there was one left." On the cover of his pamphlet of apple stories Aaron had written his name, expressing clearly that he was the author.

"Are you going to show this to the kids?" Aaron asked, eager to make his project public.

"Why don't you tell the children how you did it, Aaron. Your explanation may be clearer than mine since you made it."

Aaron's subtraction story problems went beyond the "take away" scenarios that are often associated with subtraction. In each equation, Aaron presented a set of apples divided into two subsets of rotten and healthy ones. Using the apples and apple tree as the backdrop for these set-within-a-set stories Aaron showed that he had a broad understanding of different contexts of subtraction.

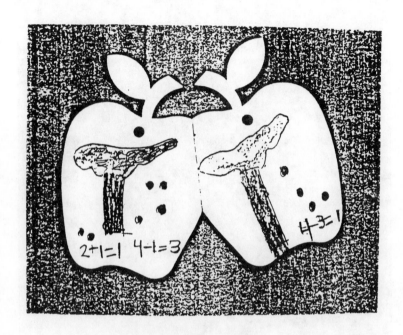

Aaron's apple subtraction stories.

FIGURE 3–4

After sharing his apple stories with the class, Tim asked if Aaron could create some addition stories using the same theme of apples. He set to work immediately, switching from subtraction to addition with ease. When asked to tell what his new apple stories meant, Aaron reported, "One apple fell down and then two apples fell down." For the second page Aaron said, "Three apples fell off the tree and two apples fell off the tree."

By publishing his apple stories Aaron proved his status as an author of mathematical ideas; he even created a cover for his pieces and bound them by stapling the edges together. His insistence on having his work shared with his peers and then bringing it home to share with his parents showed us how important publishing was to him. His use of art to reflect and extend his meaning was essential to the understanding of this piece. After sharing these projects with his peers, other children became interested in representing mathematical ideas in this way. Aaron showed an obvious pride in having his work adapted by his peers (Figure 3–5).

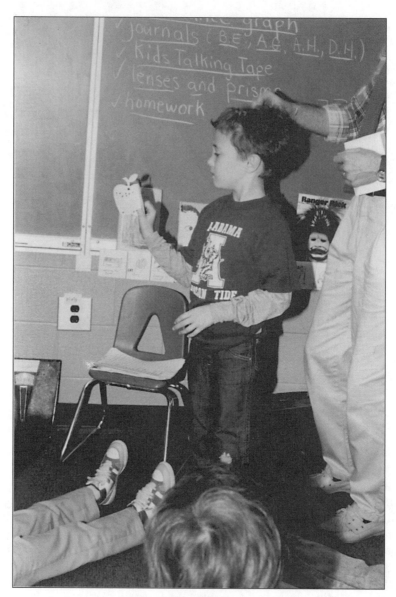

FIGURE 3–5

Using Mathematics to Tell a Boat Story

Aaron showed another example of his extraordinary creativity and imagination when he produced a fascinating and intricate story about boats, a topic that held his attention throughout the school year. Boats were a personal theme for Aaron and they showed up in many of his stories and much of his artwork. Aaron and his father loved to fish and together were saving money to purchase a modest bass boat.

This particular investigation began when Aaron completed a sheet of math facts left out in the math area. This was an independent choice that Aaron and many children often made because of a need either to improve their skills in this area or perhaps to prove to themselves that they could do it. After completing the page of problems, Aaron turned his paper over and created his own, far more meaningful, context for addition (Figure 3–6).

Aaron wrote three problems for himself in the top left corner of his paper and put a box around them when he completed them.

He pointed to two of the math facts that he created and said to David, "Look, five plus four and four plus five is nine," recognizing the commutative property of addition (changing the order of the addends still yields the same sum). Thus Aaron began a prolonged engagement with a project that, when the process is considered, we believe is a mathematical/artistic/literary masterpiece.

Aaron drew the hull of a sailing ship and a small sail on a short mast. Recognizing that his sail was disproportionately small, Aaron erased it and replaced it with a large one more able to power a vessel of this size. Speaking aloud to David the entire time he worked on this project, Aaron described his creation. After dividing his sail Aaron explained, "Now there are two rectangles. This is one sail and this is one sail." To express this idea numerically, Aaron wrote *1 + 1 = 2* on the left half of his sail. "One person working on this sail. One person working on this sail," Aaron continued, as he drew a sailor on top of each sail. "I'll put them up there and put *1 + 1 = 2*" (Figure 3–7).

David then asked, "What else can you do to continue your story?" Aaron directed his attention below deck. "I'm going to make a wash place. Hey, I'm going to have some people waiting in line too." Aaron drew a sink with three people waiting to wash. "These two people are waiting in line and this person is waiting in line." With these words Aaron wrote *2 + 1 = 3*. Next to the waiting men Aaron drew a counter with three bowls on it. "The bowls are the same number as the people in line," he commented. "Two bowls plus one bowl equals three bowls."

David was interested in how Aaron used drawing as a catalyst for creating further mathematical equations. He encouraged Aaron to continue

Aaron's mathematical boat story.

FIGURE 3–6

his story by asking, "What are you going to do next?" Then Aaron drew a person on the deck brandishing a sword. "The captain doesn't eat," he said, after putting a crown on the captain's head. Aaron quickly drew four humps in the lower left corner of the page, representing waves crashing into the bow. "Two and two equals four waves," he spoke, while writing his equation.

Recognizing the need for the crew's sustainance, Aaron drew four boxes of grain below deck; he then drew a heavy dark line and four more boxes. "These and these are boxes of grain." Aaron wrote the equation $4 + 4 = 8$, to represent his illustrations. This drawing generated Aaron's

Sailors atop the sails.

FIGURE 3–7

next idea of how the food was to be prepared. After creating a large pot with four circular shapes and a ladle, he explained, "This is a big stew pot so they can warm up the grain, and this scoops out the food." While recording his equation he commented, "This is two grain and this is two grain so this is four grain."

Aaron then focused his attention on the ship's armory. He drew a small cabin on the foredeck and two missiles in flight. "These are the rockets. Two rockets he already shot and these (pointing to the *4* in his equation) are the rockets he just did last." Figuring the total number of rockets on his fingers, Aaron recorded a sum of six. Aaron did not draw all of the rockets represented by his equation. The four rockets that Aaron mentioned had already been launched and there was no room for them in his drawing; however, he does include them in his numerical representation.

Aaron then drew a large smokestack on deck complete with smoke. "Oh, yeah," Aaron said to David, "They need a flag too," and with that Aaron designed a flag for his ship with three Xs in a small box and six vertical lines. Not willing to leave this small detail without some numerical representation, Aaron wrote *3 + 3 = 6*. He explained, "These are the long lines and these are the short lines on the flag."

Again, Aaron's work became an example to the class of what authors really do. They write about what they know and often use art to complement and extend their mathematical ideas. For instance, the topic of eating led to bowls of food and boxes of grain, and soon after he shared his work, many children were incorporating numerals and equations into their artwork. Aaron was a mathematical author who demonstrated ways to represent mathematical ideas. We had all learned from Aaron this year.

Final Reflection

Aaron was not the only child with interesting mathematical texts to share. Indeed, many of the students in this class became excited about sharing new and different ways to use mathematics. In their own way each child became an instructional leader. However, Aaron truly was a guide in this area and we chose him to be the case study for this chapter not to show what is typical but what is possible for young children when they are given an environment which allows and fosters creative engagements with mathematics.

Aaron's family moved to another district the following fall and Aaron attended another elementary school. One day in November, Aaron's mother, a teacher herself, called the school to report on Aaron's progress in his new class. He was doing well in his mathematics at school and he still continued to create interesting mathematical stories at home. During the past summer Aaron had created some diagrams of the family garden complete with measurements and scale drawings. He continued to show himself to be an author who used mathematics to fit diverse purposes and changing contexts in his life.

Aaron and the other children in this transition first-grade class were mathematical authors when they entered the room in the fall. Their interests and abilities became public property through the generous sharing or publishing of their work and insights. Discoveries were celebrated. Children took risks together by sharing and communicating. Each became more comfortable in the role of mathematical author because of the encouragement to write about personal experiences and themes. Various communication systems were used throughout the day and this was no less true in mathematics. Art, oral and written language, and even drama were used along with traditional mathematical symbols to create mathematical texts. Their projects and explorations often spanned several days, indicating their intense interest and prolonged engagement with mathematical texts. Children felt free to change their texts, add new data, delete useless information, expand, and refine their texts to fit their exact needs or convey precise messages.

Aaron helped us to see the full potential of young mathematical authors. We will always be grateful to him and see him as one of our most powerful teachers.

Table 3–1   Examining Aaron's Growth over Time

Demonstrations of Authorship	Classroom Context	Mathematical Concepts	Strategies for Understanding
Authors initiate their own investigations.	Halloween survey	Quantity, equality, inequality	Classifying
Authors reflect and revise.	Vocational survey	Quantity, equality, inequality	Matching, enlisting the help of peers
Authors write about what they know.	Bean survey	Quantity, equality, inequality	Counting, comparing
Authors initiate their own investigations.	Self-initiated dice homework	Equivalence	Counting
Authors initiate their own investigations.	"Apple Math" stories	Equivalence	Comparing, classifying
Authors use alternative communication systems.	"Boat" math story	Equivalence	Matching

Authoring Throughout the Day in Second Grade 4

Analogous to Chapter 2, we describe in this chapter a typical day in Tim O'Keefe's second-grade classroom in detail. We created this section of the book in response to practical questions about the organization of the day and the ways in which mathematics is used as a tool for learning throughout the day. Although each individual strategy is useful, the ways in which they are naturally embedded into the daily life of the classroom gives them even more potential. Examining the strategies in the context of the general curricular framework demonstrates the notion that the whole is greater than the sum of its parts.

The entire second-grade classroom at Lonnie B. Nelson Elementary School will be featured in this chapter as we share the mathematical insights that were generated on February 20, 1992. In this chapter, like the one featuring the transition first-grade classroom, we portray the richly contextualized nature of learning in this community. We chose the "typical day" format to parallel Chapter 2 and to demonstrate how Tim and his children authored mathematical ideas in another school and grade level. We chose the "typical day" format to show:

- Connections between and across curricular experiences;
- The diverse range of mathematical events that occur in a day;
- The ways in which meanings are constructed, strategies are shared, and concepts are understood;
- How the curriculum is shaped and reshaped by the participants;
- The role of mathematics in the curriculum as a tool for learning and system communication;
- How the teacher attempts to understand what children know about mathematics and builds from there by creating open-ended invitations with no entry or exit prerequisites.

We believe that together both chapters demonstrate how Tim creates curriculum with his children—how the theory comes alive when teachers encourage children to become authors of mathematical ideas. We also believe that this chapter will illustrate the ways in which the learning process we are describing is universal as it applies across educational contexts. Enjoy the day!

First Gathering

Music

"This land is your land!" Melodic voices filled the air. Tim led the group with guitar in hand while Elizabeth "played" her imaginary air guitar and Brittany "played" piano on Tim's guitar case. While both used different tools, both used consistent rhythms. The beat paralleled that of the entire group's rhythm. Tim played the first chords of the next song. Several children made fists, looked at each other and responded in concert, "Yes!" indicating their satisifaction with the decision. "The water is wide . . ."

Menu

Tim carefully put his guitar away to signal the transition. It was time for "morning business." The children gathered around their teacher on the floor in the front of the room. It was Brittany's turn to share the menu. The children made a path so she could easily move from her spot on the floor to the menu posted on the chalkboard.

"Pizza, corn, fresh fruit, and chilled milk," Brittany read with a look of anticipation.

"No wonder so many kids ordered a school lunch today," Tim responded making the connection between the number of children who usually order school lunches and lunches ordered on this particular day. "Fourteen got a school lunch and only eight brought a home lunch. I don't think that's a record but it's close." As he did so, he demonstrated the concept of average. He grounded the concept in the context of the menu and demonstrated that mathematical thinking is a human endeavor and we often use it to solve problems, describe situations, or meet our individual needs. In this case, more children ordered a school lunch than what was typical for this group of seven and eight year olds.

Stick Calendar

As Tim was synthesizing the conversation about the menu, he moved toward the stick calendar. The class was so accustomed to the order of events that had become ritualized as "daily business," they all "read" the stick calendar together as Tim placed a new stick in the ones bag. "One hundred, one ten, and two ones!" rang out from the entire group. It was their 112th day of school. These authors had become literate in mathematics through prolonged engagements. Through repeated opportunities to count the progression of school days, the children learned about place value and much more. After a brief review of place value, Tim always invited the young authors to generate insights about the particular number and strategies for calculating the equivalence of the number.

"Who can tell us something about day 112?" Tim asked. Hands shot up into the air. He called Abby up to share first.

"Well yesterday we were wondering if three odd numbers would equal up to an odd number. So would 1 + 1 + 2 equal up to an odd number?" Abby inquired referring to day 112. Queries such as this are hallmarks of mathematical thinkers.

Tim responded with a question. "Well, let's figure it out. One plus one equals two, and two plus two equals four. So do you think that two odds and an even always equal an even number?" Tim wrote the question on the board: Do two odds and one even always equal an even?

Alex was the first to react: "Well, no, because if you put one more on the even, odds always come after the even. Like if it was day 113 like it will be tomorow, you add the ones and the three and you get five."

Tim, Heidi, and David recognized that digressions such as this one are often a valuable part of open-ended discussions. They also believed that many important connections are generated by the children during such ventures. Still, Tim wanted to focus on the question at hand and so he commented, "That's true but the question is whether two odds and an even always equal an even."

Brittany was next, "One plus one is two and two plus two is four so that's even."

"Yes, you're right. So you are helping us answer the question about today's number." Tim was pushing the children to think conceptually about the question. "Do two odds and an even *always* equal an even?"

Tim invited Antwan up next, knowing that Antwan was still sorting through the difference between odd and even numbers. He believed that all children had important contributions to make to the group's collective understanding of odd and even numbers.

Antwan pointed to the ones in 112 first and remarked, "These two are even and this one is odd."

Several of his friends tried to encourage him, "You just have them mixed up." Since Kyle was one of Antwan's most supportive and informative friends, Tim asked Kyle to explain his thinking about odd and even to Antwan. Tim recognized that learning is a social process and that multiple perspectives enrich our understanding.

Kyle paused momentarily and then moved to the board with a slight smile. He had an I-have-a-good-idea look on his face. "Well, these are odd [he pointed to the ones] and this is even [he pointed at the two]. Because if you have two people and two cookies you could divide it between them. If you had two people and one cookie you couldn't divide it unless you cut it in half." This was a familiar and useful explanation for the concept of odd and even. Stories such as this grew out of discussions of children's books like *The Doorbell Rang* (Hutchins 1986). As authors of mathematical ideas, children need regular opportunities to tell stories to explain mathematical concepts. Many children nodded their heads in agreement to Kyle's explanation. Antwan was not one of them.

Looking at Antwan warmly Tim attempted to clarify Kyle's point, "Do you understand what he is saying? The even numbers, like two, you can divide equally without breaking any cookies. But the odd numbers, like one, you can't. Right?" Antwan smiled. Tim smiled, too, indicating his pleasure with Antwan and Kyle. He knew this exchange would not be the last conversation about odd and even numbers. He knew his children still had various interpretations about what these numbers meant. He would look for further opportunities for children to give additional examples, tell new stories, and venture more hypotheses. They would deepen their understanding together.

Kyle had more to share about the number of the day. "If you add 112 and 112 it would be 224. There would be two twos right there [he pointed to the twos in 224]. And then add those two twos and that equals four [he pointed to the four in 224]." Kyle was looking at the pattern of adding the hundreds digit to the tens digit to equal the ones digit. He indicated that the same strategy would be true if you doubled the entire number. As authors, they were striving to make connections, seek patterns, and generate new insights about mathematics as a communication system.

"That's an interesting pattern," Tim followed.

Andy couldn't wait to be called upon. "And $4 + 4 = 8$!" he exclaimed, following Kyle's lead. "And $8 + 8 = 16$. You could just keep adding and adding."

"Gosh, that's another interesting idea. I like the way you are using mental math," Tim said acowledging his point as well as his strategy.

Kyle jumped back into the conversation: "You can just keep adding and adding and adding!"

Heidi respected the hypothesis but wanted the group to test it a bit more before assuming a definite pattern. She asked, "If you keep adding and adding will the pattern hold true?" As authors of mathematical ideas, learners venture predictions and then fine tune them with feedback from others.

Some of the most confident children looked puzzled as they continued adding in their heads. They soon realized that the pattern would break down once they began regrouping. It is open-ended discussions such as this one that challenge the thinking of all learners.

Next, Jonathan revisited the odd and even concept. "Today is even and tomorow is odd!" he stated with a sense of accomplishment.

Tim concluded the discussion by acknowledging Jonathan's mathematical idea and discussing the group's current passion about odd and even numbers. "Very good Jonathan. It's interesting how this has all changed in focus the last couple of days into discussions about odd and even numbers." Tim's observation fascinated all of us. It was intriguing to consider the concepts, strategies, and connections that emerged over time by simply inviting children to discuss the number of the day. Throughout the year, personal observations about this number were often adopted for further investigation by the entire group. Various mathematical concepts and strategies were uncovered through rich conversations such as the one above.

One particular theme in these number discussions was the concept of time. At the beginning of the school year, the children addressed the passing of time by discussing their ages and ages of siblings, parents, and grandparents. Such discussions began around day five and peaked around day eight for children, days twenty-five through thirty-five for parents, and days fifty through seventy for grandparents. In so doing, the children were making personal connections with the daily numeral. The children also made connections between the featured number of the day and the temperature. Day thirty-two conjured up memories of cold winter mornings and the fact that thirty-two degrees fahrenheit meant freezing. On day sixty-five they suggested sixty-five degrees as perfect sweater weather. On days ninety-five through one hundred, discussions about the dreadful heat of summer emerged and the children discussed the strategies they used to seek relief from the South Carolina heat: they played in the shade or went swimming. They also addressed the concept of inequality by discussing greater than and less than when comparing the relative ages of friends and family members. The concept of equivalence and the use of expanded notation equations emerged as they began attributing names for numbers. They devised a variety of equations to represent each number. For instance, for day 77, they would say things like $77 \times 1 = 77$; $70 + 7 = 77$; $10 + 10 + 10 + 10 + 10 + 10 + 10 + 3 + 3 + 1 = 77$ or $7 \times 10 + 6 + 1 = 77$; $100/2 + 27 = 77$.

The daily stick calendar ritual provided opportunities to work with place value concretely and much more. Because of the open-ended nature of the invitation, children authored new mathematical ideas each day. Some individual ideas caught the interest of the teacher and class and so became the focus of the group's exploration for many days while others remained unique to the children who composed them. As Tim taught responsively using strategies such as the daily stick calendar, he "uncovered" the formal objectives he was expected to teach in second grade. He did so in such a natural way that mathematics remained connected to the children's lives and the world in which it operates.

Daily Business

Tim proceeded with the daily business. He announced that he had ten new books for the classroom and that they would be housed on the top shelf of the book case. Then he announced a variation in the typical format for writing workshop. Normally during this time children selected their own topics and were engaged in different phases in the writing process. However, Tim and the children decided to write their own fairy tales after an extensive genre study. Consequently, they were going to have a formal celebrating authorship session on this day to draw closure to the unit of study. He announced,

> I'm really excited about the next event—celebrating authorship! Everyone has finished their fairy tales and so we will share all of them today. [On a typical day approximately five children publish at a time so this was a significant schedule change.] We will divide into three groups with about seven kids in each group. One person at a time will read. After they are done reading, make some comments just like we usually do during celebrating authorship. Tell the author what you liked about the book or any questions you may have, such as 'Where did you get your idea?' Then write some things you like about the person's book on notes. The author will pass the book around and you can put the notes in the back. Then the authors will always have your comments. They will have a permanent record of what you liked about their books.

The children were excited. They found their books and began rehearsing for this very special event.

While reading and writing were clearly highlighted as the primary forms of communication during celebrating authorship, mathematics played a role in the organization of the experience. Tim naturally demonstrated the functional nature of division by asking the children to divide into three groups of seven. Additionally, when they began making comments about the authors' texts, the mathematical nature of fairy tales emerged, such as things characteristically occurring in threes. At times the teacher and children were purposefully learning about mathematics; they were intentionally exploring the content, structure, and processes of this form of communication. At other times they were using mathematics as a tool for learning, a tool that helped them organize, explore, and better understand the world.

Surveys

The children who conducted surveys during free choice time at the beginning of the day were encouraged to share their findings during the class meeting time. Abby had been anxiously awaiting her turn. She climbed up on the author's chair and described her first survey. "I asked some people, I didn't get everybody but this is like lunch role. I asked them what they liked best: pizza, roll, spaghetti, or lasagna. Guess which one everybody liked best."

The class responded without hesitation, "Pizza!"

Abby smiled and acknowledged their vote. "Yes. Spaghetti got two and lasagna got one and pizza got twelve and roll didn't get any."

Tim suggested, "Show it to the kids."

Antwan was concerned, "I didn't vote."

Abby reminded him, "I didn't get to everybody."

Tim commented, "If I was going to guess I would have guessed pizza before I even saw your results because when we have pizza in the cafeteria almost everyone gets a school lunch." Again, he capitalized on the opportunity to show how mathematics helps them predict and reflect upon things that matter in their lives.

Abby smiled once again and said, "Mr. O'Keefe is the only one who voted for lasagna."

Curtisha pointed to the columns, one of which had no votes, followed by one with two, followed by one with one. She noted the distinct format of the columns, "I like how you have a pattern—low, high, low, high."

Dave interjected, "Do you know something else that people really like for lunch that is not on your survey?"

Abby paused, "Um . . . hamburgers."

Antwan added, "Peanut butter and jelly sandwich."

Dave pushed them to consider what might happen if she reframed the question, "I guess what I'm saying, it might be interesting for you or someone else to do another survey and try to put all of the favorites down. See what might happen then." Dave was encouraging them to think like mathematicians. He wanted them to create new questions, to pose further hypotheses, and to understand that the questions we ask reveal only a limited amout of information. In fact, any set of data merely yields more results for learners to reshape, question, and extend.

Dave continued, "OK, would you like to share the other one you did today?"

"OK, I weighed my book bag just like Brittany did," Abby announced, making the explicit connection between her work and her young colleague's. In so doing, she demonstrated the generative nature of the curriculum. Many of the most important mathematical enterprises grew out of collaborative ventures among the children. Next, she explained her survey and the results. Holding it so that everyone in the group could see, she continued. "See, this is everybody's guess. I had my book bag and I was going around and asking people how much it weighs. Some people said a half pound and Ashley said two pounds and Kyle said one pound . . . Alex said one and one-half pounds, Andy said one and one-third pounds, Brittany said three, Laura said four, Dave said one and one-half pounds, and Heidi said one-half pound."

Laura responded anxiously, "I didn't say four, I said one," revising her first prediction based on the others' comments.

Then Abby announced the official weight using her best game-show voice, "And the real number was one!"

"Yes!" rang out from those in the group who were rejoicing in their accuracy. Although we wanted children to make thoughtful decisions regarding mathematical investigations, we wanted to discourage competition and attitudes about being right and wrong. To do so, Dave posed another question about the survey that was authored a week earlier (Figure 4–1).

"Can anybody tell me if you can remember what Brittany's book bag weighed?"

Larry was the first to answer, "Seven."

"More than seven," was the clue that Dave added.

"Eleven," came from Antwan.

Dave acknowledged Antwan, "I believe so. It was more like eleven and one-half or twelve pounds."

Tim built upon Dave's observation, "One thing about the information that Abby collected is most kids were very close, and the book sack survey last week we had some guesses that were just huge and some small and some in-between. What was the lowest?"

Abby reviewed her data and responded, "One half."

Tim continued, "What was the highest?"

Abby dropped the four that Laura had originally proposed and said, "Three."

Tim refined his observation to help the children understand the relationship. "OK, so the range was very small from the lowest to the highest."

Abby made another connection with the mathematical language Tim used. When he said small, she thought about those who used units of measurement that were less than a pound. "Some people were doing ounces," she said.

Tim lit up at the opportunity to uncover the relationship between various units of weight. "OK, so some people were using units smaller that pounds to weigh."

Dave also capitalized on the teaching and learning opportunity that had arisen. "Who here was trying to say ounces? Could you raise your

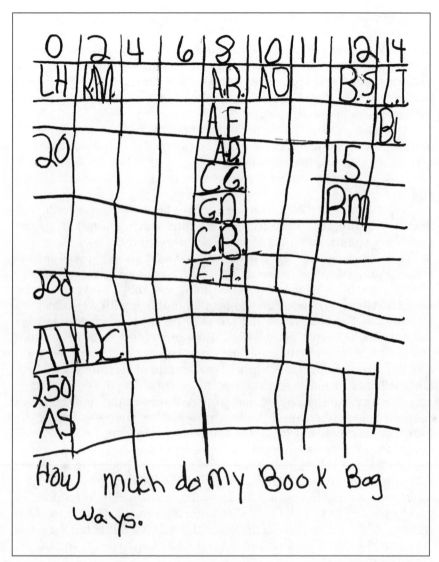

FIGURE 4-1

hand if you were trying to say ounces to Abby? Could somebody tell me how many ounces there are in a pound?"

In concert, a number of children said, "Sixteen."

Dave continued, "So, if you said it's about a half pound, how many ounces would that be?"

Alex raised his hand instantly, "Eight!"

"Eight—eight ounces. So that's another way of saying a half pound—eight ounces." Dave continued, "Another thing I noticed that people did this week but they didn't do with Brittany is a number of people used parts of a pound. Somebody said one and one half, somebody said one and one third. A lot of people used parts of a pound and last week people just said four, five, and six and so on. Does anybody know why people used parts of a pound this week?"

Kyle had an idea. "Well, because Brittany's bookbag weighed a lot more, and if it was my decision alone I'd say twelve ounces because it is very light," referring to Abby's bookbag.

"OK, when it is very light you have to use parts of a pound," Dave said.

Andy was next. "Well, you see it could be that it was a lot lighter than it was. It doesn't even feel like a pound when you pick it up and sometimes you have to use a special scale to weigh that."

Dave reacted, "Exactly. Sometimes you have to use special instruments if things don't even weigh a pound." Dave took advantage of this opportunity to make the connection between Abby's survey and the next invitation. "We have been doing a lot of things with weighing with Brittany's and Abby's graphs and Mr. O'Keefe has been measuring your weights. Mr. O'Keefe's graph reads, 'How much do you weigh in kilograms?' " We were intentionally and systematically engaging children in a variety of experiences that featured the concept of measurement. There are a number of measurement concepts such as length, weight, time, area, capacity, volume, and temperature. We wanted the children to become flexible mathematical thinkers who had an understanding of the history of measurement (standard and nonstandard units) and the relationship between measurement concepts (length, width, volume, and so on). We did not believe that it was enough for the children to know the skills involved in measurement. We wanted them to *truly understand what, how, and why we measure.* To do so, Dave planned to introduce two very popular pieces of children's literature after lunch. "I have two stories that deal with measurement. Not with weighing things but they deal with another kind of measurement. I will read them to you as soon as we return from lunch."

Invitation: Exploring Measurement Through Literature

Dave began, "The first one looks like this. It's called *The Line Up Book* and it's by Marisabina Russo [1986]. This is one of my favorite stories. It starts like this. Sam dumped out all his blocks on the floor and then he heard his mother calling him for lunch. 'Just a minute,' Sam called back. Sam started to line up his blocks. They stretched all the way across his room and out the door. When he ran out of blocks, Sam said, 'I need something else.' "

Ricky added, "Probably build his trucks next."

Dave continued, "Good prediction, Ricky. The locks lined up all the way to the bathroom. 'Come on Sam,' he could hear his mother calling. 'Just a minute,' Sam called back. He looked around. 'I need something else.' "

Several children offered suggestions: "Probably sticks. Probably pictures from the wall. Pictures, ducks, bath toys."

Dave responded, "Yeah, well those are good predictions 'cause you can see some things that he might be able to use. Bath toys." Dave read and the children chimed in making predictions throughout the book. Dave was nearing the end of the book. He read, "He looked up and there was his mother saying, 'Three.' She looked down at Sam. 'What are you doing?' she said. 'I made a line all the way from my room to you,' said Sam. His mother looked at the line. She picked Sam up off the floor and hugged him. 'I love you, momma,' he said. 'And I love you Sam,' said his mother. 'And now it's time for lunch.' "

"Aaaaagh," gasped the children delighted with the happy ending.

Dave asked, "Any comments about that story? Raise your hand if you want to say something about the story. Kyle."

Kyle said, "At first it's about measurement because, it's kind of like counting to see how long it gets."

Dave called on Abby next. She said, "Well, we could do that in our class, like, put the guitar case and stuff like that and make a line all the way over to there."

Laura remarked, "I'm going to add on to what Abby said. I was thinking we could do it this a-way and this a-way. And we can see how many blocks it takes to go this a-way, see how many blocks it takes to go that a-way. Like an inch apart."

Heidi added, "So, if you go one way and then the other, you could then determine if you used the same objects both ways whether the room is wider or longer, because you could count the number of objects."

Dave continued by reading another story about measurements, *How Big is a Foot?* (Myller 1990). In this fictitious story, a king orders a bed for his queen to celebrate her birthday (in the days when beds were not yet invented). He asks her to lie down on the floor (with her crown on, of course, because she always sleeps with it on), and he uses his foot to measure her height and width. He gives these measurements to the royal carpenter, who constructs the bed as the king requested. However, the bed is much too small for the queen, and the carpenter is thrown in jail for his incompetence. Soon, the carpenter realizes the problem: his foot is smaller than the king's foot! The story ends happily when the carpenter uses a marble cast of the king's foot to build a bed that is the correct size. The story nicely demonstrates the problem of using nonstandard units of measure.

After reading these two stories, Dave invited the children to do some measuring themselves. Children were asked to measure their height using a piece of adding tape. Then they measured their height using nonstandard units of measure (Figure 4–2), such as their feet, cubits, digits, etc.

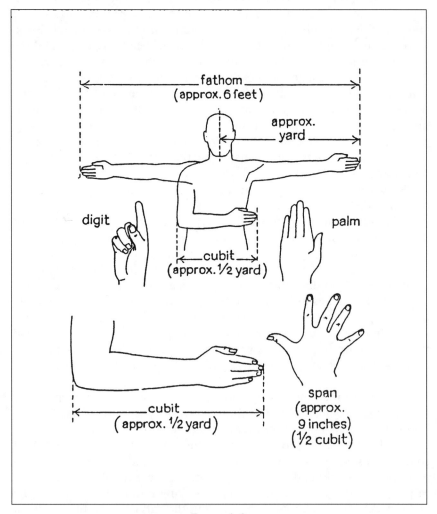

FIGURE 4–2

The Project

"I'm going to give each person one of these charts. With some adding tape, figure out how long you are, how tall you are. You may have to lay down on the floor. Then figure out how tall you are if you used *your* foot, cubit, fathom, and so on. How many of each of those would you be long? You can write it right on here," explained Dave, pointing to the tape.

Heidi overheard Kyle asking a good question and so brought it to the group. She said, "Kyle asked if two people could work together on this. It makes sense at least during the initial measurement part."

"In order to figure out how tall you are, Kyle, you will need someone to help you and then you will use your own lengths to measure yourself, such as your own span, cubit, and so on," said Dave.

The children embarked upon the project. Some moved to the book corner, others began working at a table, while others could be found scattered around the room. Although they chose different locations, we noticed immediately that *all* of the children were productively engaged in the project! They went to work right away. They were anxious to see what they would find out through this investigation. As authors of mathematical ideas, they started composing before their pencils hit the adding tape. We overheard them making predictions. "I think that my foot is the same as my cubit; I think I am taller than my fathom; I think I am five feet tall." They found partners easily as they were accustomed to working together in this classroom. They were also comfortable using mathematics for real purposes. This was not a novel opportunity to do something fun in mathematics but a reflection of the way *they lived and learned together in this classroom.*

Heidi began working with several children in the book corner. She explained their reasoning to Tim as he came by to check on their progress. "They have taped their adding tape to the floor so it won't move," Heidi said emphasizing the resourceful nature of the group. They did not need to be told exactly how to solve their problem. As soon as they realized that the adding tape moved too much to ensure accurate measurements, they began using masking tape to hold it down. Heidi continued, "Jonathan measured one span and then looked at it in relationship to the whole."

Jonathan added, "I took my hand like this [spreading it out on the adding tape] and I used it to measure the size of my foot. I tried to guess first." Jonathan had created his own measurement scale. He found that his foot equaled one span and so decided to use his foot to measure his height.

Heidi extended his point, "And he said he thinks he is seven and one half of his own feet tall and now he is checking his prediction. He is being very careful to measure exactly one foot each time." Jonathan carefully scooted his shoeless foot along the paper tape, marking its length each time with a pencil.

Heidi turned to Jonathan in anticipation, "Jonathan, you are very close." He was nearing the end of the adding tape.

Jonathan stopped. He and Laura began counting together, "One, two, three, four, five, six, seven."

Laura concluded, "Just about seven."

Heidi noticed that they had begun counting on the second foot and so suggested a recount. "Let's all try again." Heidi pointed to the first foot and they began counting together.

"One, two, three, four, five, six, seven . . . and one half!"

Heidi looked to Tim and said, "His estimate was . . ." Jonathan interrupted her in excitement.

"Seven and one half, that's what I guessed and I got it right on!" Jonathan smiled proudly.

Next, Heidi shared Laura's strategy. "Laura has another strategy. Laura marked the length of her foot on the adding tape, then she said, 'I know what I'm going to do, I'm going to get a ruler and see how long my foot is using inches.' And she found out that her foot is eight inches. So now she is using a ruler to estimate the rest of it because she thinks it would be more accurate than moving her foot across the tape."

Tim asked, "How many feet do you think you are Laura?"

Laura responded quickly, "Around a couple. It's not going to be more than three or four."

Tim posed another question to clarify her prediction, "It's not going to be more than three or four of your own feet?"

Laura said, "Yea, or five or three because my feet are fairly big and my paper is fairly big but I think it's just going to be a couple."

Deanna walked up, arms spread out, holding the adding tape from fingertip to fingertip. "This is how big my whole self is," she said while holding the adding tape vertically, "and this is how big my arms are. . . ." She held the adding tape horizontally. "This is how big my arms are all the way across to my other arm." She was exploring the relationship between length and width.

Tim reframed her explanation using the language of mathematics, the nonstandard units of measure, "So your fathom is just as long as you are tall?" Deanna nodded with a eureka kind of smile.

Tim moved to Brittany's table. "So what are you writing on yours, Brittany?" he probed.

She answered, "This is Rebecca's."

He asked again, "So what are you doing?"

She explained, "It's kind of like the doctors when they measure how big you are. They have little children's stuff on it. Little stuff like at the doctors'. It's, like, decorated."

Tim was delighted that she had made the intertextual tie between her personal measurement experiences at the doctor's office and this particular engagement. She was not simply playing; she was making connections between two distinct measurement experiences in a thoughtful way.

As Tim continued to survey the room he noticed Abby walking heel to toe across the adding tape. Next, she dropped to the floor and spread her arms out across the adding tape. She looked contemplatively at her teacher and reported, "I'm one fathom, six and one-third feet, and four and one-fourth cubits." Then she returned to her business and began crawling across the adding tape and measuring using her palms. She counted as she went. She looked up and said in a matter-of-fact way, "It's eleven palms."

Andrea was working in the same area. Tim turned his attention to her. "Andrea, what are you finding out?" Well, I'm finding out . . . um . . . what's this? She pointed to her fingers.

Abby overheard her question and referred her to the chart. She said, "Digits."

Andrea returned to the initial conversation and said, "Five digits." She continued, "This pencil is ten digits, so that's an easier way to do it."

Tim appreciated the diverse strategies the children were devising. Andrea had made the conversion: one pencil equals ten digits. Lying her pencil down on her paper strip end to end, Andrea simply counted by tens to determine her length (and height) in digits. "Good thinking, good thinking, Andrea!" Tim declared.

Although we predicted that they would respond to this invitation strategically, we were truly pleased with the range of strategies the children were developing. In this case, Andrea found a shortcut to adding up all of her digits. She found that ten of her digits equaled the length of her pencil. She then simply added by tens using her pencil instead of adding up all digits individually. Thus, she created a more appropriate measuring tool to measure her body length; digits were too small and cumbersome. Later, we related her strategy to an experience featuring centimeters and decimeters. Andrea was using her pencil as a decimeter. It is this flexible use of measuring tools to fit the context that is at the heart of mathematical literacy.

As Jonathan continued working, we noticed him creating his own measurement scale as well. He used the *length* of his finger rather than the *width* for a digit. He calculated that one of his feet was the same as three of his digits. His own measurement scale (length of finger = digit) contained equal partitions with a consistent pattern: digit, digit, digit, foot. The relationship between the smaller unit and larger unit highlighted the concept of ratio. Jonathan had created a three-to-one ratio (Figure 4–3).

Tim checked on Kyle next, "What are you finding out now?"

"Well, in my feet," Kyle said as he examined the adding tape closely.

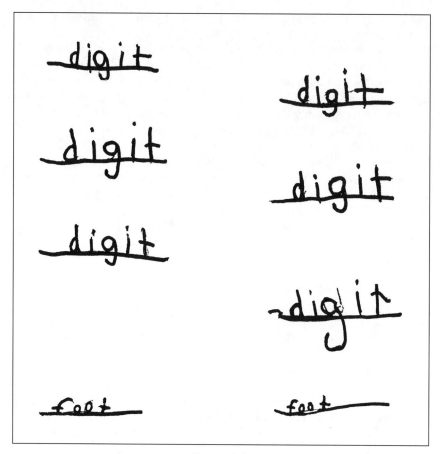

FIGURE 4–3

"Oh! I made a little mistake here." Kyle explained what happened, "It was supposed to be five, not four." He erased the four and wrote a big, bold five at the end of the adding tape. Kyle knew that mistakes were not criticized and so he felt comfortable going public with his miscue. We believed that children needed to generate and test hypotheses to grow. We had learned that children expand and refine their thinking through the process.

Tim pushed him to consider the meaning represented by the numeral. "So what did you find out about your feet?"

Kyle began tapping the lines that divided his paper with his eraser. He looked up and remarked, "It's five and one half and one third" (Figure 4–4).

Tim asked further, "Tell me what you mean by that." His response clearly reflects his belief in children as sense makers. Although Tim him-

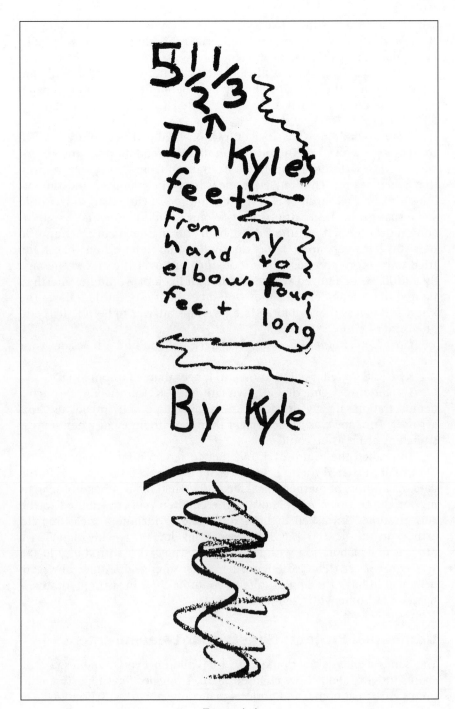

Figure 4–4

self was not quite sure what Kyle meant, he knew that Kyle's answer was the result of systematic, rule-governed thinking, and he wanted to learn more about the child's problem solving strategy.

Kyle explained, "Well, it's five cubits, and then a half cubit, and then another third of a cubit." He cleverly used denominate fractions (having 1 in the numerator, such as $^1/_2$, $^1/_3$, $^1/_4$, etc.) to describe his remaining length of tape.

Tim took note of Kyle's use of fractions and planned to use his idea to help Kyle as well as the others think about adding fractions and/or considering partitioning beyond one half and one third. We noticed that when several children were measuring their lengths and the last length to be measured was less than the measuring unit, kids would solve that problem in various ways. Some would count that length as "one more." Others counted it as "half," no matter what fraction of a part was left over, since it was clearly less than one; others, like Kyle, tried to be more precise. Kyle's foot stuck out over the end of the tape by a little, so he figured where one half of his foot would be, and then figured the remainder after that would be about one third of a foot (he knew it was less than a half). He figured his answer to be one half and one third of a foot.

Tim asked another question, "What else did you find out besides your feet?"

Kyle said, "Well, really I know I'm longer than a fathom long."

Tim inquired, "One of your own fathoms?" Kyle answered through a demonstration. He lay down on the adding tape and spread his arms across it. The tape was in fact longer than his fathom even when he was stretching as far as he could.

Tim called the group back together to reflect upon the experience. The children shared their personal results and looked for patterns in the data. As authors of mathematical ideas, they had made a habit of searching for connections. After most of the children had contributed to the conversation, Tim asked if they would like to include a measurement activity in the next *Weekly Newsletter*. (Tim devised weekly homework projects in collaboration with his students. They were introduced in the *Weekly Newsletter*.) The experience had been so engaging that they were delighted to have the opportunity to continue their measurement investigations at home with their families.

Homework Project: Nonstandard Measurement

Tim sends a newsletter home with the children every Wednesday. He shares insights about how children learn, strategies for supporting children's growth at home, and projects that connect work at school to life at home. On Wednesday, February 26, the newsletter grew out of the group's current experiences in reading and mathematics.

Dear Parents:

I have seen a lot of progress in all of the students this year. They have grown socially, emotionally, in their ability to understand mathematics, in their ability to read and write, in their speaking ability, listening ability, etc. Growing and changing are inevitable. Some of the children have clearer understandings of some subjects than others but all of them have strengths and abilities.

This week I'd like to write a little about how children read and how they show us what they know about the reading process. They can give us a view about what they know about reading by reading to us aloud. When children read to us they show us what they think reading is. Interestingly, when children make mistakes or "miscues" they let us in on their reading strategies. We can tell a lot about their strengths and weaknesses by listening closely. For example, if the child reads and it sounds like a word list it may be that they are "word calling" and not really understanding what the print means. A way to find this out for sure is to discuss the reading. If the child is reading and comes to an unfamiliar word s/he will do various things. Some children will call a word that looks like the word on the page but does not make any sense in the piece being read. ("Tom and Ann walked down the straight." FOR "Tom and Ann walked down the street.") If the child does not recongize that there is a problem with the meaning then this shows us that s/he is *not* reading for meaning. This child focuses more on word calling than the meaning of the piece. Others will say a nonsense word that looks like the word being read. ("Tom and Ann woke doon the street.") This child is focusing on the phonics or letter sounds and not really listening to the meaning of the piece. Other children may miscue by substituting a word that may not look anything like the word being read yet makes sense in the sentence. ("Tom and Ann walked down the road.") This last child is making the kind of miscue that indicates that s/he is really paying attention to the meaning of the passage being read. If you were to pick one of the children from above as the best reader of the group, who would you pick? You probably would pick the one who miscued by substituting another sensible word. We can see that this child is making meaning from the process. The others show poor strategies that, when taken to the extreme, really interfere with understanding print. Next week I'll give some strategies you can use to help with reading.

Last week the children did some great activities with measuring using nonstandard units of measure. Ask your child about the measuring we did in class. For this week's homework I would like the children to use the same units (fathom, digit, cubit, palm, span, foot) to measure some things around your house. The children are to create their own chart showing the measurement of at least ten things from home using the units on the attached sheet. They are familiar with this sheet and will probably teach you a thing or two about measurement. Please try other measurement activities at home with standard and nonstandard units. Don't forget your comments on your child's work.

Thanks for reading!
Tim O'Keefe

The children collaborated with their parents and siblings and expanded and refined their understanding of measurement in doing so. They also taught their family members along the way. They had several days to complete the project. They returned the results of their investigations with comments from their parents on Monday. Tim strongly believed in genuine collaboration with his children's parents. He encouraged them to document three positive comments and a wish or a goal for their child (Mills and Clyde 1990). This strategy invited parents to make observations about their children and share them with Tim. He valued their input and often published their comments in follow-up letters. This framework promoted genuine collaboration and helped children make connections across learning contexts. Andy measured a variety of objects at home and recorded his observations on his "Measurement Chart." Andy's mother observed and supported his efforts and then documented her observations (Figure 4–5).

We were intrigued with the children's responses and the stories they told about their measurement experiences at home. When we asked them to reflect upon what they had learned from that particular homework, Abby responded, "Everybody, I even asked my grandma. I said, 'Do you know what palms and cubits are?' She said, 'Nope.' I asked my mom and she didn't know what they are, I asked my brother and he didn't know what they were. I mean they need to go back to school I think." While Abby's comment amused us, it also revealed an important feature of a sound mathematics curriculum. It is important that mathematical thinkers understand *what, how, and why* we measure. It is important that they have regular opportunities to use nonstandard units of measure so that they see a need for a standard and also gain a historical perspective of our measurement system. We have found that understandings such as these come through explorations where authors pose questions, venture hypotheses, encounter anomalies, make predictions, and share ideas with others. By adopting an inquiring stance, children learn mathematics while using it to explore and understand their world.

Reflections

We hope we have highlighted the children's mathematical investigations throughout the day so that, as a reader, you could vicariously experience

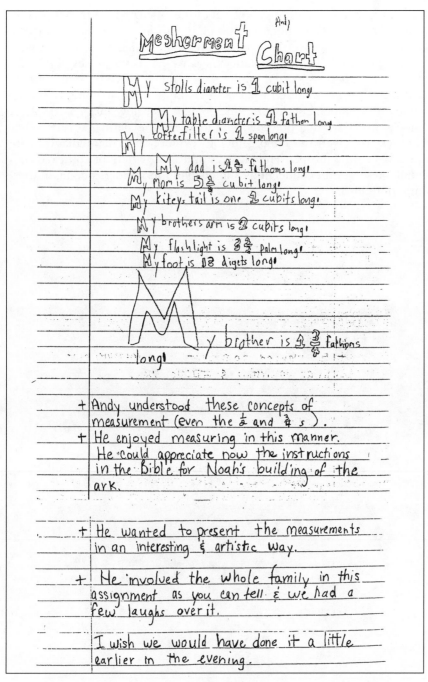

Meshermen**t** (Andy) **Chart**

My stolls diameter is 1 cubit long.

My table diameter is 1 fathom long.
My coffee filter is 1 span long.

My dad is 2½ fathoms long.
My mom is 3½ cubit long.
My kiteys tail is one 2 cubits long.

My brothers arm is 2 cubits long.

My flashlight is 3½ palm long.
My foot is 13 digets long.

My brother is 1¾ fathoms long.

+ Andy understood these concepts of measurement (even the ½ and ¾ s).
+ He enjoyed measuring in this manner. He could appreciate now the instructions in the Bible for Noah's building of the ark.

+ He wanted to present the measurements in an interesting & artistic way.

+ He involved the whole family in this assignment as you can tell & we had a few laughs over it.

I wish we would have done it a little earlier in the evening.

FIGURE 4–5

and appreciate the learning potential of the curriculum. We developed a chart like the one at the end of Chapter 2 to tease out significant incidents. In so doing, we illustrate the ways in which the children were learning to think like mathematicians as well as key features of the curriculum that best supported mathematical literacy. We have also identified the strategies children used to develop an understanding of several important mathematical concepts. When perusing this chart, please imagine the days that preceded and followed this particular one. When children are given the opportunity to explore such mathematical concepts over time in open-ended ways and in a variety of contexts, they build a reservoir of connections and deepen their understanding of these important ideas.

Table 4–1   Reflecting on the Day's Events

Demonstrations of Authorship	Classroom Context	Mathematical Concepts	Strategies for Understanding
Authors solve problems.	Menu	Average	Counting, comparing, predicting
Authors grow through prolonged engagements; authors share their texts; authors tell stories.	Stick Calendar	Place value, equivalence, temperature, time, and inequality	Counting, noting patterns, predicting
Authors share their texts with others and celebrate their growth.	Celebrating authorship	Ratio and equivalence	Partitioning
Authors share their observation and texts with others, authors use alternative communication systems to reflect and extend.	Sharing surveys	Weight	Predicting
Authors initiate their own investigations; authors share their thinking in diverse ways; authors make intertextual ties between current text and past experiences, and authors create novel texts.	Measurement using nonstandard unit.	Length, equivalence, ratio, and proportion	Predicting
Authors use alternative forms of communication to collect, organize, and display data; authors initiate their own investigations.	Measurement homework	Length	Measuring, estimating

The Investigations of One Author Throughout Second and Third Grade: Sara 5

Sara Sharnoff is a student in Tim O'Keefe's third-grade class at Lonnie B. Nelson Elementary. As we write this in mid November Sara has been in Tim's classroom for one and one-quarter years. She was in his second-grade class last year and when he was given the opportunity to teach another grade he opted anxiously to go to third grade with most of the same students he had taught in grade two. While this is not a revolutionary practice by any means, he has never had the chance to follow a group of students for two years. The experience is wonderful.

This chapter is a case study of one student. We are writing it for the same reasons we wrote about Aaron from the transition first-grade class. At times, a close look at individual students may shed light on the learning that occurs across students.

We cannot write this chapter about Sara Sharnoff, the mathematical thinker and author, without also writing about her as our friend and teacher. As much as anyone, Sara has helped us to see what is important in teaching, learning, and living. Before getting to know Sara as a mathematician, we think it is important that we introduce her as a citizen of the world, to explain what she cares about, and the kinds of things on her mind.

Sara is a breathtakingly good writer. She has helped the class see the value of poetry, to attempt new genres such as mysteries, and to make connections between the kinds of materials she reads and what she writes.

At the end of the last school year (Sara's second-grade year), Tim was reading Lois Lowry's *Number the Stars* (1989). While we hadn't finished it when the end of the year came, we managed to read over half of this compelling novel about two friends living in Denmark during the Nazi occupation. Lowry's book had a profound effect on all of us, but it had a special effect on Sara and her friend Julie. Perhaps it is because these friends are Jewish or maybe it is simply the strength of the writing that made Sara and Julie connect so much to the story. When it became clear to everyone that Tim wouldn't have enough time to finish reading the book, Sara and Julie wrote this poem in first person to sum up their feelings:

War

I hate war. It is bad. It makes me feel angry, tingly, and mad. Bombs are dropping on every house. We are inside tossing about. We have no food, we have no clothes, we have to stand there in a shivering pose. The house smells bad—too bad to say. And just think I stay here everyday. The poor little girl, tears down her cheek—the poor little girl could not even speak. We heard footsteps beneath the door—we thought about death and even more. But they came to free us. Freedom rang through our ears and through our tears.

We have chosen Sara as the case study to represent second and third grade not because she is the fastest or most accurate student in the class on computation; she is not. We did not choose her because she is an uncanny problem solver. While she is very good, she was not, for example, chosen to be in fourth-grade accelerated mathematics as three others in the class have been. We chose her because she demonstrates drive and determination (a word that she herself uses to describe her learning), the willingness to help others, and a clarity of voice that makes her a wonderful learner and a teacher of other children and adults. Sara demonstrates potential.

Analyzing Data

The class had always had an interest in creating and analyzing graphs and surveys. Tim invited participation in this kind of project from the first day by asking about transportation to and from school, the practical information needed to keep track of the children's whereabouts during the day. Various attendance graphs, interest surveys, and questionnaires were being conducted on a regular basis and the children actively participated in their analysis and discussion. After setting the tone and allowing the students to see the potential of this mathematical experience, the students took over and often chose topics, selected appropriate methods of data gathering, formatted their findings, and presented them to the class. Part of regular classroom business was the presentation of this work. The children authored these graphs and surveys alone or coauthored with one or more classmates.

While Sara always cooperated with her peers who were gathering data, she was rarely one to create a graph or survey on her own. Her strength came in the analysis during group time. Always sitting in the front of the group, Sara added insight and extended the range of interpretation of the data. Typically, after the group would tell what we could notice merely by looking at the data—finding patterns and performing simple computation—Sara would ask, "Who would like to know this information?" As an author, Sara wanted to know what audience would find these results helpful. It was a question that she kept raising throughout the year.

In February of second grade the class was studying the states of the Pacific Northwest. Tim brought in four different kinds of apples all grown in Washington for the children to sample. The tasting was completed and the students' choices were graphed. The four apples were pictured across the top and the names of the children were written in columns below their favorites.

Amy noticed a pattern in the children's responses, "I saw that in most of them there's a pattern, girl, girl, boy, girl, girl, boy. In number four there's a pattern too. Girl, girl, boy, boy, girl, girl."

Jr. wanted to discuss similarity in taste. "I thought Red Delicious was the same as Gala because they tasted alike. The Jonagold and the Granny Smith tasted more alike too."

"That's an interesting connection," Tim noted. "They also look more alike."

"I think that Gala was really nasty," Courtney interjected, eliciting chuckles from the class.

"Apparently four people disagree with you. They thought it was their favorite of these four," Tim reported.

Hart replied, "OK, see column four minus column two equals column three."

"Mr. O'Keefe, I know who would like to know this information," Sara said, adding a practical twist to our conversation, "A baker. Because then he would have to know. . . . Say people were complaining about sour ones. He might say I won't use the Granny Smith, maybe I'll use a Gala or a Jonagold. So it'll help him decide what to think. So for apple pies or something like that he might have more information."

Sara's statement changed the course of the conversation as she did so many times. Courtney said fancy chefs would need to know this. Hart suggested buffet-style restaurant managers, and Amy noted that grocery store owners would alter their produce selection based on this type of information.

Sara was going beyond the information in front of the class and extended this invitation for analysis and discussion beyond the classroom. This characteristic of a mathematical author was her trademark during the analysis of this kind of data. The question she raised was a useful one because it helped the class appreciate the human dimension of mathematics.

Authors of mathematical ideas not only gather and display data but they envision the different audiences who might find this data useful in some way. Sara was helping us to enlarge our sense of audience.

Only a week later, we were reviewing all of the stories read as a class for a literary unit on fairy tales, and a class graph was created for the question, "What is your favorite fairy tale?" During the discussion period that followed, Sara again went beyond simple observational comments— " 'Rumplestiltskin' has the most," or "If you add 'Snow White' to 'Cinderella' it equals 'Rumplestiltskin.' " Sara was pushing herself and her classmates by introducing different kinds of concepts into the discussion.

"Look at 'The Three Little Bears' and 'Rumplestiltskin.' If you look at the number in these columns and columns in between, it's two, one, one, one, two. It's symmetrical, the same on both sides. It's kind of like a palindrome. Two, one, one, one, two. If you turned them around it would still be the same."

By introducing the concepts of pattern and symmetry, Sara elevated the conversation in a sense by inviting others to go beyond the simpler inequalities and short equations.

Sara offered other thoughts later: "A doctor's office would like to know this kind of information, 'cause in the waiting room people just get so bored. The office people should know which kinds of books they should have for people who are waiting." Sara's practical application of the data grounded the question in the world of waiting rooms and restless patients, providing a real purpose for this information.

At the beginning of third grade, only a week after school started, Jeffery created a survey on the question, "What's your favorite pizza?" After surveying the class Jeffery shared his results at the next class meeting. After most people had responded to the numbers Jeffery collected in statements—"Pizza Hut has three more than Domino's," and, "If school pizza had two more it would be equal to Domino's"—Sara once again raised the question of practicality.

"I've got two kinds of people who would like to know this information. One is the people who work at Bi-Lo or Food Lion [local grocery stores] because they would need to know what is the most popular to put out to try to influence buyers because if more people like Domino's-type pizza they would know what to put in each aisle."

"So you would want to put out the pizzas that are more like the popular ones," Tim replied.

"And the other one is the people who make snack bars," she continued. "Because they might want to know what kinds of foods people like. My brother, he was trying to find a way to make extra money and he was thinking of doing something like a snack bar. He would have to know what kinds of foods people like and what kinds they don't like."

"So you would want to have a pizza on your snack bar that is closest to Pizza Hut because that's the one more people like," Tim said.

Because Sara would often find a reason to use the kinds of information generated by the graphs and surveys from the classroom for real-world application, she gave more purpose to this kind of project. The question generation and the data collection, formatting, and presentation are more than enough reason to encourage graphs and surveys. But the insightful, functional analysis by Sara and her classmates elevates these tasks from a simple project to a complex, open-ended opportunity for students to extend, pose questions, raise issues, and take risks—all characteristics of authors of mathematical ideas.

Mathematical Storytelling

Students who are generating and solving mathematical problems demonstrate the ease in which they can communicate through the language of mathematics. Tim constantly provided opportunities and invitations for the students to challenge themselves in this way. When time was a focus of study, Tim would ask the children to create "time stories." When measurement was being studied the children wrote and drew about measurement. The creation of story problems through art, written text, numbers, and numerical expressions was known to the class simply as "math stories."

Through their math stories Tim could come to know the students better as mathematicians. Sara was particularly fond of math stories and would often create them when she had free time in class and even at home.

Sara's first two math stories had to do with a lady buying pets from a pet store, a story rather like those found in textbooks. In her problem from August 25, Sara's lady buys two dogs, three cats, and a bird (Figure 5–1). Her equation has multiple addends, which is slightly more complex than stories submitted by many of her peers. She uses the word *altogether*, a term frequently found in mathematical story problems, to describe her final sum.

Nine days later, Sara's math story included three addends like her first story but also contained a second part where the lady returns the puppy, thereby reducing the total number of pets by one (Figure 5–2). Sara revised her equation two or three times to match her writing and decided to show the lady acting on the decision to reduce her number of pets by drawing a leash in her hand. The lady's intentions are clear. While Sara's story was simple, she cleverly orchestrated her tale with her equation and artwork to create a cohesive mathematical text.

In November the class was exploring money. Tim put some coin stamps and a stamp pad in the math area and invited the students to

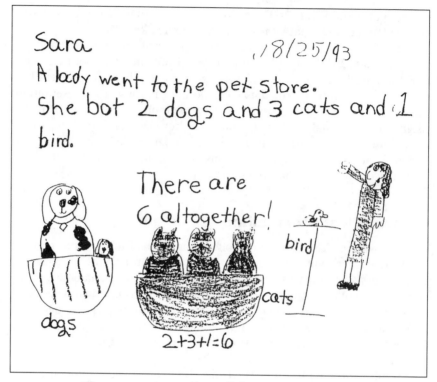

FIGURE 5–1

create math stories with them and then share the stories with the group. Sara found time right away to create two mathematical texts. The first is an uncomplicated story about a boy who had some money and wanted more for his piggy bank. In this story Sara stamped four dimes for what the boy had and three dimes for the ones he found.

In her second money story, Sara wanted to show some purchasing and had to figure out a way to use the coin stamps with subtraction (Figure 5–3). Since her girl started with fifty cents Sara stamped two quarters. Sara placed a minus sign between her quarters and the four dimes it cost the girl to buy the candy. The change, two nickels, is stamped to the right of an equals sign so her coins represent exactly what is written in her equation. Creating a number sentence with the coin stamps was an intriguing challenge that inspired several children to create similar number stories with the coin stamps.

Two more money stories were inspired by Tim reading *Alexander Who Was Rich Last Sunday* (Viorst 1978) and the poem "Smart" by Shel Silverstein (1994). After sharing some literature about money, Tim asked

Sara   4-3-93

A lady went to the petstore she bott.....
a cat and towdogs and a bird. She returnd
the puppy. Now she has a bird a cat and a
dog.

$$1+2+1=4+1=3$$

FIGURE 5–2

everyone to write some money stories. Sara's stories tell much about her
as a mathematician. Her first involves adding to determine the amount of
money she has, adding to determine the cost of what she wants to buy,
and subtracting to find out how much she has left after her purchase. Her
picture matches her text with the cashier seen from an interesting perspective. There were multiple steps in this story. She had to regroup on
two of her equations and was concerned with decimals and cents signs.
The context is simple but the mathematics is rather complicated.

A week later, Sara took another approach to the same invitation.
This story is all about context—a boy who cons his friend into giving him
money for a toy that he doesn't buy. The mathematics is easy and all
done mentally. There is no need for an equation (Figure 5–4).

Through these stories Sara demonstrated real competence for authoring in mathematics. Sara showed that she was comfortable with the
computational aspect of money as well as being adept in giving substance
to her story. It is not very likely that either of these stories would parallel
the kinds of word problems found in a math textbook for beginning second

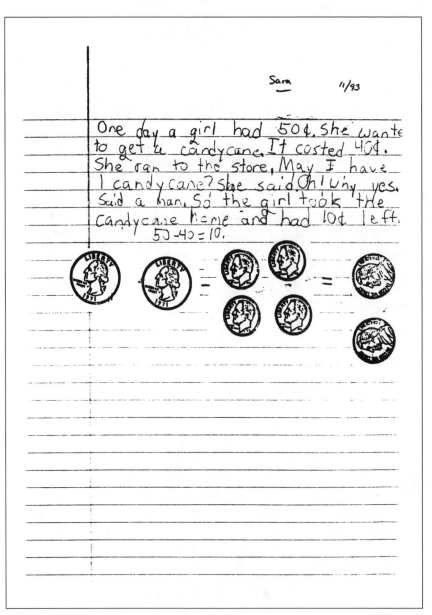

Sara   11/93

One day a girl had 50¢. She wante
to get 4 candycane. It costed 40¢.
She ran to the store, May I have
1 candycane? She said. Oh! why yes.
Said a man. So the girl took the
candycane home and had 10¢ left.
50 - 40 = 10.

FIGURE 5–3

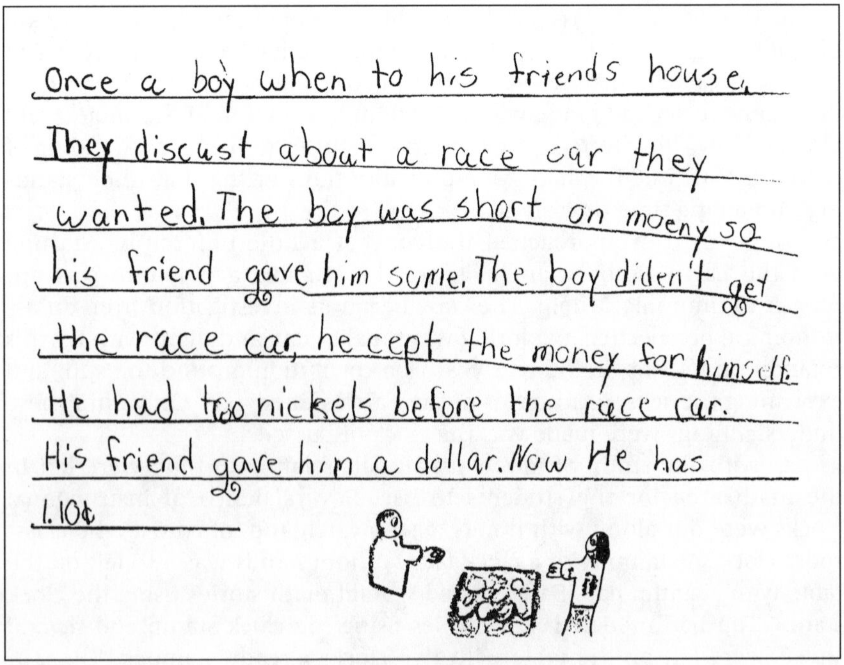

Once a boy when to his friends house.
They discust about a race car they
wanted. The boy was short on moeny so
his friend gave him some. The boy diden't get
the race car, he cept the money for himself.
He had too nickels before the race car.
His friend gave him a dollar. Now He has
1.10¢

FIGURE 5–4

graders. Sara's first story is probably too complicated, involving two different operations and regrouping with addition as well as subtraction. Her second story gives many more details than the story problems typically found in mathematics texts. To Sara, the reason for mathematics is precisely *because* of the stories. The rich context for Sara's story not only shows her as an author of mathematical ideas but an even better author than that of the mathematics textbook found in her classroom.

While working on a project for the *Weekly Newsletter*, Tim was inspired by Sara's math stories using the coin stamps. He decided to ask everyone to create some money stories at home. Sara was asked to write another story using the coin stamps to use as a demonstration for the newsletter. This scenario was reduced and reproduced in the newsletter. Once again Sara carefully used writing, artwork, numbers, and the coins to create a context-rich story to show the potential of this activity.

All of the customer's money is shown between the girl and the pet store owner. Then the four dimes are carefully divided between the girl and the pet store owner, with each indicating what is "mine." The cost of the fish is posted on the fish tank and the six dimes in the lower right corner are divided into what she has left (twenty cents) and what she started with (forty cents).

In March, Sara's class focused on the concept of time (that is, the skill of telling time as well as understanding the relative passing of time.) Tim had always felt that time was a difficult concept to teach. Several children came to second grade with a good understanding of the subject and already knew how to tell time. Others had an intuitive understanding of the nature of time but had some difficulty transferring that understanding into telling time on a standard clock.

This year Tim approached the concept a little differently. Starting with the Earth's movement in space, he felt like a whole-to-part approach to time might help. The class began its investigation from an astronomical perspective, exploring what makes day and night with Earth's rotation on its axis, defining a year as a revolution around the sun, and explaining the seasons in terms of the Earth's tilted axis. Only after these understandings were made was the clock discussed.

As with the study of money, materials relating to time were left in the math area for the students to use. Several kinds of instructional clocks were out along with timers, a stopwatch and, of course, the classroom clock. A stamp with a clock face without hands was also left on the table with a stamp pad. Sara created several math stories using the clock stamp. Tim had modeled time stories using the clock stamp and several sheets were left on the table with two clocks already stamped. The students could use these in a story to help show the passing of time. Sara caught on quickly and on the same afternoon created three stories including before and after times and an amount of time that has passed.

Sara demonstrated an understanding about the passing of time and a logical way to show it in her story. Incorporating her wish fulfillment about staying up well past her bedtime, Sara recorded the difference between the time she was "supposed to go to bed" and when she finally made it by drawing the hands on the clocks. While she was responding to Tim's invitation, Sara's story was all her own.

Another math story involving time followed quickly and involved something else personally meaningful, quilt making (Figure 5–5). It is what Sara invested personally that makes these stories her own. While her classmates all had unique stories to tell—some realistic, some completely make-believe—Sara demonstrated to her peers and to her teacher the ease with which she could tell a mathematical story.

Sara often initiated her own mathematical authoring by becoming enthused about a science topic or a piece of literature. In the following story she used both as sources of inspiration. During the period when Tim was reading a chapter book to the second-grade class called *The Prince of the Pond* (Napoli 1992), there was an intense interest in frogs. This delightful fairy tale describes what happens to the Frog Prince between the time he is magically turned into a frog by a wicked witch and

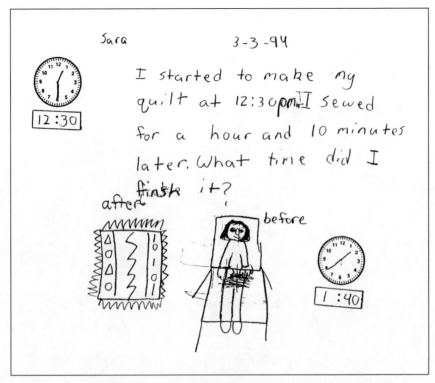

Sara   3-3-94

I started to make my quilt at 12:30 pm. I sewed for a hour and 10 minutes later. What time did I finsh it?

FIGURE 5–5

when he is turned back into a prince via the kiss of a princess. It enchanted the children and coincided nicely with a holiday gift to the class from one of the students. Monica brought in a tadpole hatchery kit that contained a coupon for frog embryos. Everyone in the room was looking at the world like a frog scientist. Sara took a character from the book named Jade and created a scenario about lost and found eggs (Figure 5–6). Sara used round numbers and did the math in her head, but the fact that she accessed information she was learning from a fictional book demonstrates how freely she borrowed information from another author to create her own text. Sara engaged in the creation of math stories during her extra time, time she could have used to read, listen to stories at the listening center, play mathematical games, conduct surveys, and so on. She very often chose to create math texts during her free choice time.

On the back of Sara's frog story she created another, more complicated, math story involving multiplication. (Figure 5–7) This story took a little more thought, and Sara revised several times by erasing and rewriting

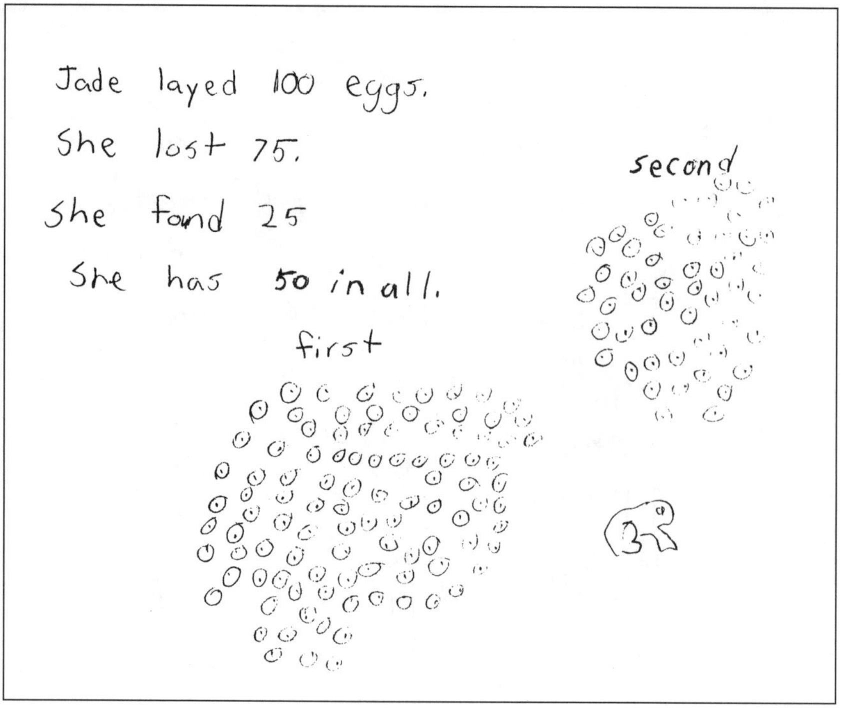

Jade layed 100 eggs.
She lost 75.
She fond 25
She has 50 in all.

first

second

FIGURE 5–6

before she was finally satisfied. In her first frog story she was careful to draw the exact number of frog eggs she began with and what she finally ended up with after losing seventy-five and finding twenty-five. In her second story only a fraction of the trees are pictured and the tree frogs falling are only symbolized by the lines coming from the trees. Because she turned to much higher numbers, the artwork became more abstract and symbolic.

Sara's stories tell much about her as an author of mathematical ideas. At times, she created her own math texts, as with the frog stories. At other times, Sara responded to open-ended invitations with originality and personal connections. By choosing to create mathematical stories on her own, Sara showed us that she was an inquirer whose work was never done. Art played an important part in some of her stories, while in others she included art merely as an afterthought. Just as her writing took many forms from nonfiction to nature poetry to mysteries, Sara's mathematical texts were also diverse. Sara was clearly one to put sense over symbol. To her, mathematics was a language for storytelling.

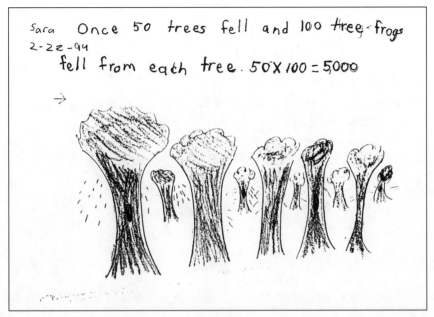

Sara Once 50 trees fell and 100 tree-frogs
2-22-94
fell from each tree. 50 X 100 = 5,000

FIGURE 5–7

Sara on Theory

Sara was constantly showing us what a flexible thinker she was. In January of her second-grade year, during a follow-up discussion inspired by a book about dinosaurs, Sara wrote down some thoughts that she had about theory. She explained at a morning meeting, "It's sort of good that we've got so many theories, because if there was only one theory then everyone would get so used to it and then if someone had some new theories everyone would think that it wouldn't be possible because they were so used to the first theory that they couldn't change their minds" (Figure 5–8).

In Sara's illustration she pictures two people arguing about the colors of the moon and rocks. Two very important words on the bottom of her work let us see quite clearly the power of her young mind, "Who knows?" Sara showed the class in her modest way that one shouldn't become too comfortable with current knowledge because that knowledge is often tentative and rapidly changing. What was once held as truth is subject to scrutiny and change and so one needs to be open minded. Sara's words on theory might serve mathematicians and scientists of all disciplines. Not being able to "change their minds" keeps people from growing and accepting new ideas. As a second grader, Sara saw some things more clearly than many adults. Taking risks, posing new questions, and

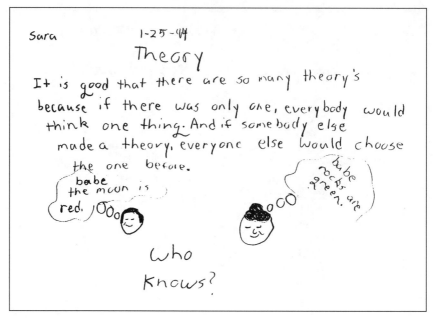

FIGURE 5–8

being open to a wide range of options are qualities of authors of mathematical ideas. Sara clearly showed us these qualities.

Interviews with Sara

On June 1, 1994, only a few days before the end of the year, Tim asked Sara if he could record some of her notions about mathematics. The question Tim focused on in this interview was, "What is mathematics?" Never one to be short of words, Sara gladly agreed to discuss what she was currently thinking about. During a recess time in late spring, Tim taped a conversation with Sara. A few excerpts of that conversation follow.

"[Math is] something that we can use to make the world a lot easier and a lot more simple place to be. It really helps people in their jobs. If there wasn't any math then no one would know what they are talking about. Everything would be a big jumble. It makes things a lot easier. Like when you have to go to the grocery store and you have to know how much money. That's math. Really you don't just need math in school. You use it everywhere."

Sara realized that mathematics is much more than a subject in a classroom. By saying that without mathematics "everything would be a big jumble," she pointed out that mathematics is indeed a language with which to communicate.

When asked about how children learn mathematics, Sara responded, "Just by talking about what you're learning really gives you a good start. It makes a big difference." Sara knew that mathematics classrooms should not be quiet places but environments where ideas are shared and problems are posed and answered within a group.

Sara was then asked to describe some of the mathematics in her life. "There are different kinds of math. There's the math like two plus two. That's the kind of stuff you find in books. But there's math all over. *Even though you can't see it, it's still there. You can just feel it. There's math there.*"

Asked to clarify her last statement Sara responded: "Like when I was getting ready for my birthday party, we had to measure from one corner of the room to the other for putting balloons up. Maybe it wasn't just numbers. . . . I didn't see five plus three anywhere, but still that was math. It wasn't shown there but it was just there."

Sara then offered some more of her family math. "When me and my family were going out to Florida we were just wondering about things that you could see. We were wondering about the license plates. You know how you can order words on them? How many were regular and how many with words? We also wondered how many trees we'd pass on our trip."

"Another time we were coming back from somewhere in a plane. Me and my dad were both sitting by the window. And we were wondering how many cars were red. What color of cars has the most? We found out that red was the most popular and that green was the least popular. I didn't see numbers on the cars but that was math. Just thinking about it. That was math. The feeling of math was there."

Sara and her family wondered about the world and used mathematics as a tool for asking and answering their questions. It is not important how Sara determined the most popular car color or even if she was close to determining how many trees they passed in a given time. What matters most to Sara, and what should matter to teachers of mathematics is "the feeling of math."

The following interview took place on November 11, 1994, while she was in third grade. It is tempting to analyze the conversation Sara had with Tim but it would probably be good for readers to draw their own conclusions about mathematics instruction and the nature of mathematics as seen through the eyes of this eight year old.

TIM: Have you thought any more about mathematics? How we use it in our lives and what it means?

SARA: I think it's more like a feeling than a subject in school. 'Cause if you actually thought about it, everything you look at is math. It's more than just pencil and paper. Everything you see is really math.

TIM: Can you give me some examples? You say math is a feeling. I'm not sure everyone would understand that.

SARA: As I said, math is really everywhere so . . . I'm looking around the classroom. Like the clock over there is really a feeling because you're looking at it. It's something that you usually would always look at that's got numbers. Time is also an element of math.

TIM: What do you think is the best way to teach math? What sort of things would you suggest to teachers as good ways to teach math?

SARA: For a real little kid who was just learning numbers, take subtraction. If a problem was maybe five minus two, I would go two . . . three, four—and the answer would be out on your fingers. If it's addition, like five plus two, you'd go five . . . six, seven—and it would come out of your mouth, but you'd be using your fingers to figure it out.

TIM: So you think it's OK for beginners to use their fingers.

SARA: Yeah—I think that's the easiest way for kids to learn. Really if they just practice counting—if they just look at something—if there's like six plants. If they just practice then they would really learn math.

TIM: Any other advice you might give to someone who was thinking of teaching math?

SARA: I would just say allow the kids to make as many mistakes they can because if you keep correcting them every time they make a mistake they are never going to learn. I think I'd give them a few blocks or something to count and make up math problems.

TIM: So, you think it's good for children to use a lot of real stuff like blocks and fingers. I'm intrigued by the idea of mistakes. How is it that you think mistakes help you to learn?

SARA: Let's say there was a problem that you needed to know seven plus three, all right, ten. Say maybe by accident they skipped nine—then maybe they'd learn the next time they did it when they figured out that their answer was wrong. I think if they get it wrong they'll be more determined to make it right.

TIM: So realizing that you made a mistake might make you more determined. That's a lot like writing. If someone doesn't know how to spell something we go ahead and encourage him to spell it the best he can. Then when he might see it . . .

SARA: Then he'll try to remember it the next time.

TIM: Right. Let's say it's being edited by an outside editor or if they see that word somewhere else—just the fact that they realize they may not have gotten it the first time, that might help them to attend to it more the next time they want to use it.

SARA: Determination really makes it a lot easier. Like when I was learning how to read. This really did happen to me. My brother was learning how to read. I must have been in kindergarten. He was in third grade. I got *so* jealous because I wanted to read *so* badly so I could catch up with him. It was easier for me to learn because I really wanted to do it. But I think if I really didn't want to do it, it really wouldn't come to me as easily.

TIM: As a teacher how could you help that person get that determination to learn the way you describe?

SARA: Well, just letting them practice and letting them do and think on their own. If you just give them a piece of paper and you just say, "Figure things out"—it's going to be harder for them. I think if they figured out things just looking around, I bet they'd find a lot of math things just sitting right there.

TIM: Just using the real world?

SARA: Yeah, 'cause there's a lot of fake stuff—stuff in books—I really don't believe in that. I think if you really look around the world you're really learning something else also while you're learning . . .

TIM: I agree! You're learning all of the time whether it's math facts or whatever. Just being a citizen of our world you can't help but learn a lot. So determination, making mistakes, teaching using real things. Think about our classroom for a second. What are some of the things that we do this year that you think are real math?

SARA: Using the checkbook ledger and looking through the toy catalog. [These were two of the mathematical projects the class was involved in at the beginning of grade three.] That's something we're going to want to know when we grow up. How to really *use* numbers. That was real math I think.

TIM: Anything else that comes to mind?

SARA: Well, you know writer's workshop is also great because I think writing and reading also have something to do with math. That's something *real*. These books we've been publishing have been really great. . . .

TIM: Perhaps that helps with that determination that you were talking about, just wanting to do it and having workshop helps you to do it.

SARA: The math stories we did for homework were also real math. We figured that out on our own.

TIM: You created the problems, you solved the problems the best you could. I must admit that a certain amount of what I plan is probably not real math.

SARA: But that's good practice and that's what I also said.

TIM: You have to strike a balance between those pencil-and-paper activities and those things that are more like using the catalog and the checkbook ledgers. Any other thoughts that you have on math?

SARA: Well, if I was a teacher I would let my students make mistakes and learn from them. I don't know how you would make a child want to learn. A certain amount of practice would help them to understand more and I think they would probably like that a lot better.

TIM: So the more they do real things probably. Too many pencil-and-paper tasks . . . timed tests, math book pages, test, test, test. Too much of that might turn someone off to math.

SARA: Kind of a mixture of both.

TIM: I like what you said about writing. Can you make any more connections with that? With reading and workshop?

SARA: Reading is also good. That also gets them more to have more determination. I think writing—with writer's workshop, that really makes a big difference. I don't really know how that connects with math but I think somehow reading, writing, and math somehow always kind of connect together . . . three main subjects and those are the most important things to understand math. I call them all one group because they are really bunched . . . those three.

TIM: It occurs to me that when we work with real math we must do a lot of reading, not just reading problems but reading situations and then trying to apply math to them. Of course with writing, if you want to describe something to someone, and that person isn't right there, then writing seems to be the way to do it. Whether you'd do it with a pencil or sitting at your computer. Expressing yourself, being able to read and understand things that you can apply math to, being able to write and explain things. I think all of these are really important.

How I've Changed This Year

While the purpose of this book is to highlight mathematics, it is *learning* that we are interested in and how best to allow children to teach and learn from each other, the environment, and—yes—the teacher. The teacher has the responsibility to create a classroom that is stimulating, yet open to change; projects that have purpose, yet are open ended enough so that all students may participate, and be successful; a structure that is predictable yet flexible enough to encourage spontaneity and wonder; and a curriculum that works within the confines and guidelines of the school and district, yet is creative and free enough to allow all participants to feel ownership and pride in its direction. It is the balance of what must be done and what should be done that is the art of teaching. This art must be found within each person who enters the classroom as a teacher. It cannot be learned from a book, but perhaps it can be learned from our students.

As Diane Stephens (1990) says, as teachers we must continually ask ourselves what really matters. Sara may give us a glimpse of what really matters in her final reflection on the last day of school when she was in second grade (Figure 5–9).

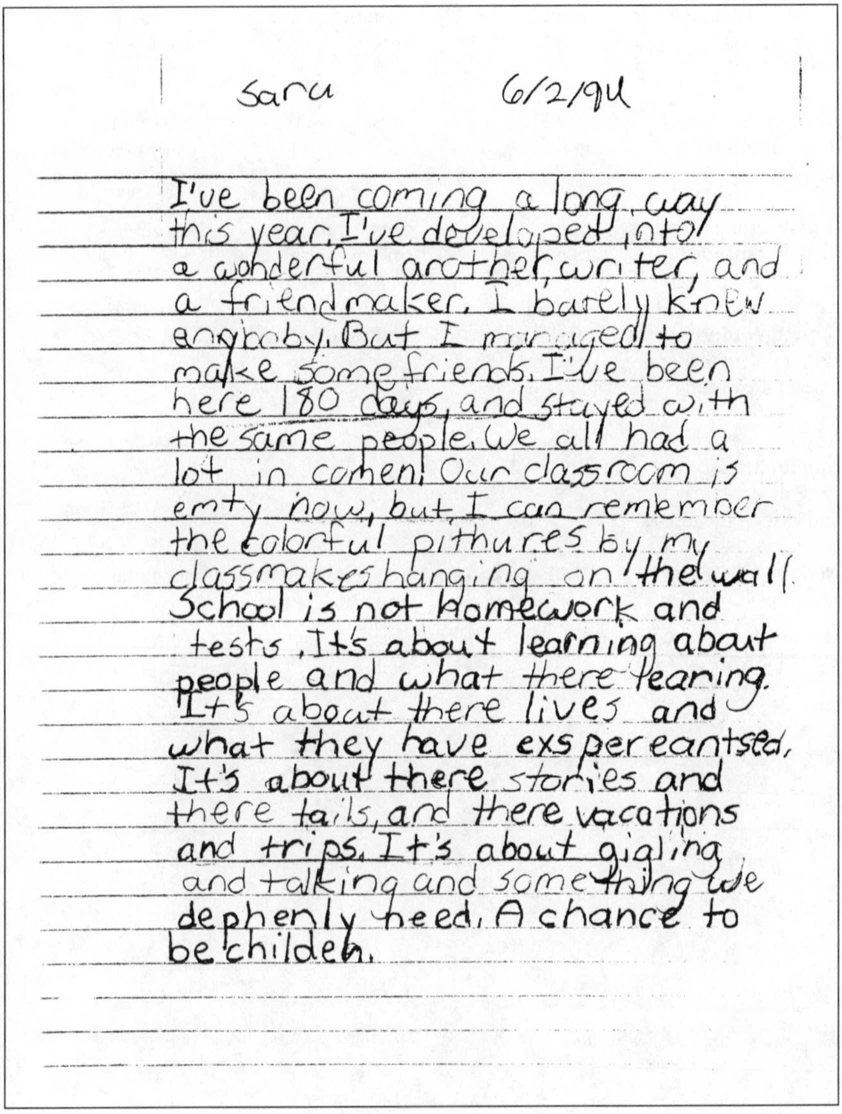

Sara   6/2/94

I've been coming a long way this year. I've developed into a wonderful arother, writer, and a friendmaker. I barely knew anybaby. But I managed to make some friends. I've been here 180 days, and stayed with the same people. We all had a lot in comen! Our classroom is emty now, but I can remember the colorful pithures by my classmakes hanging on the wall. School is not homework and tests. It's about learning about people and what there tearing. It's about there lives and what they have exspereantsed. It's about there stories and there tails, and there vacations and trips. It's about gialing and talking and something we dephenly need. A chance to be childen.

FIGURE 5–9

Table 5–1   Examining Sara's Growth Over Time

Demonstrations of Authorship	Classroom Context	Mathematical Concept	Strategies for Understanding
Authors share their observations with others.	The apple graph	Sets	Classifying, ordering
Authors share their observations with others.	The fairy tale graph	Symmetry, pattern, sets	Classifying, using deductive logic, predicting
Authors share their observations with others.	The pizza graph	Sets	Classifying, ordering, using deductive logic
Authors initiate their own investigations.	Math Stories of pets	Sets, equivalence, and numeration	Counting
Authors use alternative communication systems to reflect and extend meaning.	Mathematical stories of money	Sets, equivalence, and numeration	Counting
Authors use alternative communication systems to reflect and extend meaning.	Mathematical stories of time	Time	Using deductive logic, comparing
Authors reflect and revise.	Mathematical stories of frogs	Sets, equivalence, and numeration	Matching

Exploring Concepts over Time: Infinity Strikes Again

6

We have demonstrated the ways in which children in two classrooms developed an understanding of various mathematical concepts over time. We have also documented the evolution of mathematical thinking in two children. In this chapter, we will focus primarily on one very intriguing mathematical concept. We will show the diverse ways that children explored the concept of infinity throughout the year. In so doing, we will highlight the importance of revisiting concepts over time and the ways in which infinity helped the children better understand other units of study such as ecology, the universe, and time. Although mathematics textbooks often "cover" topics in a specific order and for predetermined periods of time, we will show how this notion is not always in the best interest of the class. In fact, the children were the ones who promoted conceptual thinking in depth and helped us see how limited it is to cover a concept for two weeks and then move on. This chapter focuses on the importance of conceptual thinking and highlights the significance of following the children's lead when creating curriculum.

The Beginning

It was Gordon who first brought the concept of infinity to our attention while he was playing a subtraction game with Tim and some of his second-grade classmates on September 24. Each person in the group had a stick of ten Unifix cubes. In this subtraction game, the children took turns rolling a number cube with the numerals zero through three printed on the faces of the cube. The object was for the children to take turns subtracting the number rolled from their stick of ten cubes until everyone had zero cubes. From the beginning of the game the students were making in-process observations and predicting outcomes such as, "If I take one away, I'll have an even number," and "I bet he gets down to zero first because he has the least amount." Gordon raised some probability assertions before the game had gone very far. "There's more of a chance for me to go out first. The only way for me not to go out first is for me to get lots of zeros, and that probably won't happen.

When the game was complete Gordon mused, "This game could go on forever, you know."

"How?" Tim asked.

"Well, if you had enough [Unifix] cubes, like millions and millions and millions of 'em. Or if you could keep rolling zeros forever and ever."

"Are there any other ways it could go on forever, Gordon?" Tim asked, genuinely interested. It was clear that Gordon was reaching far beyond the basic subtraction his teacher had intended. His interest in possibilities and extensions piqued Tim's curiosity.

"Well, if you had a number cube that had all zeros on it, it could go on forever." Gordon was considering the concept of infinity two different ways. He was thinking of an infinite quantity (his use of "millions and millions and millions" indicates this) and an infinite number of non-moves (continuously rolling zero and/or using a cube with zeros on all of the faces).

This exchange touched off an exploration on the concept of infinity that involved the entire class for the rest of the school year. Gordon led the way as this class of second graders explored, pondered, mused, argued, and defended their notions about this abstract idea.

Exploring Infinity: Conducting Research with the Children

As a teacher-researcher, Tim began asking how ideas that emerge in the classroom develop and become focused over time. Why did certain topics and concepts keep emerging while others—which the teacher valued—seemed to stay in the background?

During this school year Tim noticed that certain themes kept playing themselves out in many contexts throughout the curriculum. While several concepts gained status, no concept was more intriguing to his students than infinity. From games, to book covers, to the investigation of symmetry, to discussions about the nature of matter, the universe, and time, infinity kept appearing. "Infinity strikes again," became the class rallying cry that marked each new insight about infinity.

While Tim was also interested in the notion of infinity, he was most intrigued by the kinds of connections the children made with this concept in vastly different contexts. Was there something inherently interesting about the topic, or was it the treatment of it that captivated the class so much? The children enjoyed finding examples of situations that seemed to have this never-ending quality. Sharing most children's fascination with dinosaurs or very large numbers, these children may also be inherently intrigued with the magnitude of large things, such as the countless stars in the sky, or the inevitable, unending march of time. Midway through the year, Jonathan's mother remarked to Tim, "All he ever wants to talk about at home anymore is infinity. What did you do?"

What Made the Difference: Following Gordon's Lead

Tim frequently invited the children to share important insights with the class. Intrigued by Gordon's notions about this concept in regard to Unifix cubes, Tim asked him to describe his thinking to the class. Tim suspected the fact that he encouraged Gordon to go public with his ideas gave this concept a certain prominence and perhaps contributed to its popularity.

Tim began, "We were playing 'Make Zero' with the Unifix cubes. During the game Gordon said the game could go on forever and I asked him to explain what he meant. He said that one way it could go on forever is if you kept rolling zero all the time. Then it would last forever because you would never get to take any cubes off of your stick. Another way is if you had millions and millions of cubes. That could take forever too if you had so many that you could never get to the end. A final way is if you had a cube with all zeros on it. Yesterday we were reading *The Lorax* (Geisel 1971) in our literature study groups and Andy and I were having a written conversation. I asked Andy what I thought was a hard question, 'Do you think that one truffala seed could change everything back to the way it was before?' Andy, tell the kids what you said."

Andy said, "Well the truffala tree could grow and you could eat a fruit and plant that seed and keep planting and eating and planting and eating until you had a whole patch of truffala trees." Tim responded, "That made me think of things that could go on forever."

Next, Dave Whitin shared some books with the class that involved the concept of infinity. He felt stories would be another powerful avenue for children to make connections with this concept. He read aloud *Hot Pursuit* (Moerbeek and Dijs 1987), a never-ending story that features a knight chasing a dragon, which is chasing a troll, which is chasing a witch, and so on until the story returns to the original knight and the never-ending chase begins again! Dave concluded the book at this point and asked the children to respond.

Erica said, "It goes over and over. We've already gone through the whole book. It goes over and over and never ends."

Andy added, "You could read it for the rest of your life. If you kept following the arrows it would go on forever and ever."

Gordon said, "It keeps going in circles."

Dave confirmed Gordon's idea: "Yes, a lot of people say a circle is a shape that never ends."

Elizabeth said, "It seems like a circle, square, and a triangle keep going on forever.

Erica provided a concrete example, saying, "You see it's just like if you are out somewhere. There's a big rock and you might be going around it and around it and you might just think you're going around and you're getting somewhere but then you'll notice, 'Hey! I'm just going around in the same place!' "

Christopher concluded the discussion with another example: "I have something that will go on forever—stars. It's just like a whole bunch of stars in the sky."

Dave then read another book, *Beyond the Hill* (Ekker 1985) that portrays infinity in a different way. Again, he looked to the children to begin the interpretation.

Erica said, "It goes on and on and one of them says, 'Does it stop there?' and it keeps saying, 'No, no, it doesn't stop there.' The world never ends. Nothing can end. It's sort of like in that book. That's what we're talking about."

Andy added, "If you took a rocket ship from the earth you could go on for the rest of your life and never stop."

Christopher pondered, "The universe never stops. It just goes on forever. I don't know why it goes on forever but it does."

Becky remembered what she had learned during the ecology unit and remarked, "It's sort of like trees because there's a tree and it might fall down but another tree will start to grow and it will never stop because another and another and another tree will grow."

Gordon wondered, "It's hard to imagine never stopping. You can imagine other things in your mind but you can't imagine never stopping . . . just going straight on and on. If you took a rocket ship off the earth and you went straight sometimes the world might take you around in a circle and there might be things in space that you might run into. There would be lots of stars and you would have to dodge them, and that would make you turn and then you'd come back and then you would go everywhere around."

Gordon, Becky, and the others' comments were quite impressive for a first formal look at such an abstract concept as infinity. They pondered as young philosophers, struck by the awe and wonder of the infinite. The children touched on infinity as a repeated cycle (the life cycle of trees), a closed loop (the book that you could keep turning around and reading), an immeasurable amount (the amount of stars), and an immeasurable distance (the immense nature of space in the universe). Words and phrases such as *over and over, never ends, forever and ever, keeps on going, goes on and on*, and *never stops* show us that these young minds already had a strong intuitive understanding of this subject and they truly seemed excited to share that understanding. Once we named the concept and invited children to make personal connections, a host of investigations and interpretations flourished.

Extending Invitations

From this point on the students were invited, formally and informally, to share their thoughts on infinity and to share examples they had discovered. Often, students built on each other's ideas. Their discussions turned to debates as they struggled to improve and defend their suppositions. In their examples the children included pieces of art, games created by the class, circular story lines found in literature, musical symbols, and many others. Perhaps they found comfort knowing that there were never any fixed answers to the questions being generated and that each example led to new questions and connections. The children asked thoughtful questions and generated sophisticated hypotheses. By creating a curriculum that encouraged the children to ponder further, the children connected the notion of infinity to author studies, the study of the human body, ecology, the use of microscopes, fractions, and many other topics.

Second-Grade Theoreticians

One of the most interesting features of the infinity study is the degree to which these seven and eight year olds became theoreticians. Many of their examples and explanations included the word *if* or phrases such as *it could be* or *perhaps*. Through these discussions the students had to be precise in their language but sensitive to nuance.

Several days after the whole-group discussion on infinity, Abby made a connection between a game created by the children and her current notion of infinity. The "Wizard of Oz" was a board game devised by the students and patterned after the novel by L. Frank Baum (1903). Miniature Oz characters followed the Yellow Brick Road as the players rolled the dice. There were plenty of built-in dangers, some of which were created for the specific characters: "Dorothy loses her shoe, go back five"; "Fire! Scarecrow go back ten"; "Everyone else but the witch go back five"; and "Poppy field! Dorothy and the Lion skip one turn."

As Abby was playing the game with some friends, she noticed a problem. She landed on a square that read, "Glinda sends you forward three." But when she moved her piece (the rubber Scarecrow) according to the directions, she landed on a space that stated, "Trees throw apples at Dorothy and Scarecrow! Go back three." "So you see," she explained to

Tim, "it's like infinity. You could keep going back and forth forever." The children who made the game had inadvertently placed these two sets of directions in opposition to each other. It was determined by the group of children playing the game that the rule must be changed. "Otherwise you might run back and forth forever and never ever be able to stop."

When Abby brought her example to the attention of the group she demonstrated her ability to think theoretically. Of course, no one would spend much time moving a playing piece back and forth simply because of an oversight on the part of the game's creators. But Abby knew there was a common interest in infinity and saw this as an opportunity to expand the group's understanding. Although Abby's playing piece was not actually caught in a closed loop of going back and forth forever, she imagined that the present situation could be like infinity if she kept landing on those same two squares. This and other examples of infinity met with a great deal of excitement from the group. These first instances served as a challenge to the other children to see infinity in unusual settings.

A week or so later, while we were engaged in a Bill Peet author study, Abby noticed another example of infinity contained within the story line of *Zella, Zack, and Zodiac* (Peet 1986). As a young ostrich grows, he continually tries to repay the zebra for saving his life. Finally, the zebra becomes a mother and the ostrich saves her young one's life. When the story was finished, the children were asked to tell what they thought about it. Abby waited patiently for her opportunity to answer and responded, "The story is kind of like infinity." When asked to elaborate, Abby said, "It could just keep on going. Zella saved Zack from the wild animals around. Then when Zack grew up and Zella had a baby, Zack saved that baby." At this point in Abby's explanation most of the class understood the internal, circular story line she was suggesting and nodded their approval. Abby continued, "It could be that Zack might have a baby someday, then that baby might be in danger too. Then Zodiac [the baby zebra] might save him. Then Zodiac might grow up and have a baby in danger. Then Zella's baby could save it too. It could just keep going like that forever!"

Abby's observations and clearly worded explanation of infinity in the Oz game and the Bill Peet book encouraged us to look for theoretical examples of infinity in experiences all around us. We were encouraged to look beyond what was there and search for infinity in new places.

The Infinity Study Grows

During math workshop, when the children made choices among various mathematics experiences, Heidi Mills offered to guide a group interested in making an infinity bulletin board. The invitation was devised to help children clarify their notions about infinity and, as authors of mathematical ideas, publish them via the class bulletin board. Heidi simply asked the children to share, through art and/or writing, their current interpretations of infinity. The group published their work by unveiling the bulletin board during the afternoon gathering.

Heidi began by saying, "The first thing that people did was to make drafts. They drew pictures to represent ideas. After that, they shared their drafts and sometimes changed their ideas or added some. These pictures represent some of their ideas."

Deana pointed to her picture of a forest and said, "If you cut one tree down then another one will grow. And they keep growing and growing and growing."

Heidi added, "So what she has here are trees that are full grown and ones that are growing. Alex made a good point. He said that as long as we don't clear cut we're OK because then each season trees can grow. Andy, tell us about yours."

Andy said, "It seems like the earth keeps going around and around forever."

Heidi referred to his picture and commented, "So this is the earth and Andy used arrows to show that the earth keeps spinning around forever." She turned to Mark next.

Mark answered, "I drew about snakes."

Heidi clarified and extended his statement: "Some of the kids in the group said that snakes have baby snakes and when snakes grow up they have baby snakes and on and on. That's why Mark decided to draw all these snakes."

Mark added, "Yeah. And I drew the sun too."

Heidi looked to Alex, "OK, Alex?"

Alex said, "Well, I have a little writing with mine. I really wanted to say that if you kept recycling something over and over it would never stop and it would be infinity."

Heidi noted, "He drew a recycling center. My favorite part is the recycling sign. He made the recycling sign out of cans to represent his idea."

Elizabeth was next. "Well I did some stars and I did 220 stars. I counted them as I did them."

Heidi explained, "She only has 220 stars because that's all that would fit on the paper. To Elizabeth the stars represent infinity." Heidi went on to share her work: "I got my idea from Chris. Chris changed his mind from using batteries to something else. Chris suggested that I make a rechargeable battery. Chris, tell us about yours."

Christopher lit up, "See, I made something about fish. See, like one fish turns around and has babies. Then they keep growing up and having babies."

Heidi shared a group-generated insight with the class, saying, "We had an interesting discussion about the snake and the fish. If these animals become endangered then the natural cycle would be broken."

Gordon concluded, "Some fish are endangered species!"

As authors of mathematical ideas, the children used art to represent the great diversity in how infinity can be conceptualized. All of the students' ideas have validity and, while some may not actually show something that is infinite (scientists might argue that there is a finite number of stars, for example), the degree to which they could theorize and create a visual representation of their ideas and justify them gave us a glimpse of the powerful potential of this type of exploration. The artwork shaped their thinking in generative ways. It pushed them to show the diverse ways infinity could be conceptualized. It helped them connect the concept to their study of ecology and the universe. As they were creating, they were constantly theorizing, confirming, and revising their thoughts on the subject. They were asking mathematical questions and using art to convey their ideas in uniquely compelling ways. The combination of art and mathematics encouraged them to create new thoughts and new ways to think (Eisner 1981).

Exploring the Evolution of Education: Infinity Strikes Again

One afternoon Heidi was eating lunch with the children when Erica asked, "Why do you and David come into our class every Thursday?"

Heidi explained, "Because we want to know how you learn best. We need to know how you learn so we can help your pen pals [undergraduates at the University of South Carolina] learn how to teach. You help us learn how to teach better by letting us work with you. Then we go back to the university and share what we have learned with our students."

There was a pause. Then Erica remarked, "Hey, that's like infinity."

Jonathan was sitting across the table. He added, "Infinity strikes again!"

Heidi inquired, "What do you mean?"

Erica said, "Well, I am showing you how I learn and if I grow up and become a teacher then I will have other children help me teach and learn and some of the children I teach might be teachers and it would go on and on, like infinity."

Heidi continued, "What an interesting idea! Would you share it with the class after lunch? Maybe you could write it down for us so we won't forget exactly what you mean."

As Erica explained (Figure 6–1), "If the teacher taught kids and the kids grow up and [were] teacher[s] and taught kids it would be like infinity. Because it would keep going, it would be like infinity." On her picture Erica drew a teacher pointing to a chalkboard and a small picture of that same teacher as a child. Through the windows one can see hundreds of stars,

Erica

Wednesday, November, 13, 1991

Good morning

If a teacher tot kids and the kids growe up, and wasateacher and tot kids, and it wauld be like infinity. Becuas It would kepe goning it would be like infinity.

Infinity

FIGURE 6–1

which was another symbol of infinity for the class. In the bottom right corner, Erica finished by drawing a recycling symbol, yet another graphic design implying something that could go on forever. Her connection to the concept of infinity also demonstrates the important role that a classroom community plays in developing ways of thinking. Infinity was becoming a class theme, a regular accompaniment to the way the children looked at the world.

Erica shared her piece at the following group meeting, and it was decided to make the sharing of these insights a regular feature on the list of business conducted each day. By making a formal sharing period each day for thoughts and ideas about infinity, the children were challenged to participate in whatever way they wanted. It was not a form of competition. Some children wrote their names on the board regularly as part of the early morning business. Others simply watched and cheered their peers on when a particularly interesting or new way of thinking about infinity was brought to the group's attention.

Exploring Infinity Through Music

By February, the class had compiled quite a list of examples of infinity. Almost every day one or two students would offer something to keep the study of infinity going. It had almost taken on a life of its own at this point. While singing "This Old Man," several of the children wanted to create other verses to make the song longer. Andy introduced the term "eternity" to the class with his suggestion that we sing, "This old man, he played eleven, he played knick-knack back to seven." "This way," Andy said, "you could keep singing for eternity. You could just keep going from seven to eleven and back again, over and over" (Figure 6–2, top).

Now that the class was thinking about infinity through music, other ideas sprang forth having to do with songs. It was the custom of the class to write down ideas for infinity sharing time on small pieces of paper and bring those to the group meetings. Jonathan, who brought forth as many examples of infinity as anyone in the group, had his name on the board and a note on the chalkboard next to his name. "I was sitting at home thinking of infinity over the weekend," he began. "I was thinking of that song [that begins] "Do, a Deer." You know how it says, 'That will bring you back to Do.' If you keep doing that you would sing it infinity times." Indeed, if you take literally the line of the song that Jonathan was referring to, you could get lost in an infinite musical loop (Figure 6–2, bottom).

Several days later, Elizabeth brought in an instance of infinity she discovered while she was attending her piano lessons. When she came into the room that morning, Elizabeth happily waved a piece of music around as she put her name on the board to share. "You won't believe this one Mr. O'Keefe," she said with a big grin. "This one has two things having to do with infinity!" She took a small note from a pad and documented her ideas. When it was her turn to share, Elizabeth was obviously very pleased with herself. "First, let me read the words," she said proudly. " 'I'm growing up and when I'm grown, maybe I'll have kids of my own. If I have kids, what will they be? Maybe they'll play music like me!' [Figure 6–3]. So you see the words are kind of like infinity. The kids could keep growing up and having kids who play music! There's also something with the music. When there's dots at the end that means go back to the beginning. So it's sort of like infinity. You could just keep going and going." On her note for sharing, Elizabeth drew the repeat sign musicians use to indicate when to return to an earlier section in the mu-

When you get to eleven
on this old man
you go
back to seven

eturnity!!!

Andy - 2/20/92

Jonathan
3/2/92

TEACHER NOTES

you saing
doo A deer
and it
sed you
came dak
tadoo and
then you

can soning
It infoty
time

"I was sitting at home
thinking of infinity over
the weekend..."

FIGURE 6–2

FIGURE 6–3

sic to play again (Figure 6–4). This symbol usually means repeating a section only once but Elizabeth was extending the meaning by imagining "What if we kept repeating that part of the song every time?"

Andy, Jonathan, and Elizabeth proudly showed the class how infinity can be figured into the dimensions of music and song lyrics. These three illustrations exemplify how this abstract concept can be shared by young children in various contexts. By being aware of infinity, the children saw it in many different circumstances. By being encouraged to share their findings the children became researchers, philosophers, and teachers.

Exploring Infinity Through Art

There were also several examples of infinity found by the children in art. The first one, which encouraged all of us to look for examples in artwork, was shared by Jonathan. While reading *101 Wacky Facts About Mummies*

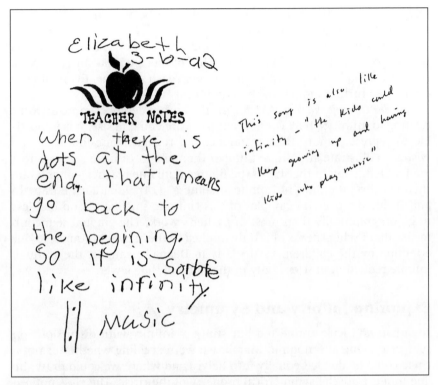

Elizabeth
3-6-a2

TEACHER NOTES

when there is dots at the end. that means go back to the begining. So it is Sorbt like infinity.

|:| Music

This song is also like infinity – "the kids could Keep growing up and having kids who play music"

FIGURE 6–4

(Harris 1991). Jonathan noticed the cover of the book. "Look, Mr. O'Keefe! Another example of infinity!" Jonathan explained to the class, "There's this picture of a mummy reading a book. The book that he's reading has a picture of the same mummy reading the same book. So it looks like infinity strikes again!"

This clever example is not as apparent as it seems at first. The book that the mummy is reading does show the same mummy reading the same book, but in the smaller book the bottom half is not completely drawn for the reader to see. Jonathan inferred that if one could see the rest of the smaller book, it would also have a picture of the same mummy reading the same book and so on.

Yet another example of infinity in artwork was discovered by Deana in the unlikely context of Pizza Hut 3-D glasses. On her note for sharing, Deana wrote simply, "My glasses from Pizza Hut." On the paper glasses frame, there is a picture of a child wearing 3-D glasses. Even though the small picture of the boy does not clearly show any other design on the glasses frame he is wearing, Deana inferred that the boy in the picture, if he was wearing the same glasses, would also be wearing a picture of himself on those glasses, and so on.

These three children clearly built upon each other's ideas. There was no jealousy or selfishness with ownership of specific ideas. Insights were celebrated and lots of oohs and aahs greeted each new one. Every discovery invited further inquiry in this community of learners.

In *The Graphic Work of M. C. Escher*, the author describes more artwork relating to infinity: "If all component parts are equal in size, it is impossible to represent more than a fragment of regular plane-filling. If one wishes to illustrate an infinite number then one must have recourse to a gradual reduction in the size of the figures until one reaches—at any rate theoretically—the limit of infinite smallness" (14). Jonathan, Elizabeth, and Deana discovered examples of this "infinite smallness" and had less to go on graphically than most of Escher's work. The gradual reduction in size that Escher speaks of is only implied in the artwork brought to our attention by the children. Particularly in Deana's example, the gradual, infinite reduction in size is only in the mind of the viewer.

Exploring Infinity and Symmetry

Jonathan and Kyle connected our study of infinity with discussions on symmetry. One afternoon in March, we were deciding whether or not a circle could be divided equally into halves and where we could draw the line to illustrate the symmetrical property of the circle. The class noticed that if you divide the circle horizontally across its center it would demonstrate that the circle is indeed a symmetrical shape. Soon it was determined that as long as one draws a straight line across the center of the circle it evenly divides the circle. Tim could see Kyle contemplating the situation very carefully. He posed the question, "So, how many times do you think we could divide this circle symmetrically?"

"One hundred!" offered Antwan.

"I'll bet at least a thousand," said Larry.

"What do you think, Kyle?" Tim asked. He didn't have his hand up but Tim could tell that he had been thoughtfully studying the situation.

"Infinity times!" was his enthusiastic response.

"The chalk doesn't make the lines small enough to make more than about a hundred lines before the whole circle is filled in," said Tim.

"Yeah, but we're not talking about the chalk lines," Kyle declared. "We're talking infinity!" The others agreed after some discussion about lines and what they represent. As authors of mathematical ideas they were exploring theory in this second-grade classroom.

During the same discussion about symmetry, Tim had drawn a rectangle on the board and asked for a volunteer to draw the lines that would divide the shape into two equal parts. Jonathan noticed that if a person drew a line vertically across the center of the rectangle it becomes a smaller rectangle which could then be divided horizontally to create yet another rectangle, which could be divided again and again. He declared that you could, "keep folding it infinity times and that it would just keep getting smaller and smaller."

Without any direct definition or explanation on the teacher's part, these two boys, with the help of their classmates, made clear a very abstract and hypothetical notion that mathematical lines do not take up space even though their visual representations do. Without the concept of infinity in the forefront of the class' collective mind our investigation into symmetry would not have been as rich. By knowing that infinity was a concept that could help them better understand their world, the class valued any further examples of infinity. Jonathan and Kyle helped us view symmetry in a more accurate and complete fashion while adding to the collective knowledge of infinity as well.

Many Contexts for Infinity

Numerous examples of infinity came up throughout the school year. Our interest in infinity never dissipated. The students saw infinity at the barbershop when sitting between two parallel mirrors, in physical education games when the children were tossing a ball across a circle to a different partner each time, in T-shirt designs, in the circulatory and respiratory systems when we were studying the human body, in astronomy when we were discussing the moon's orbit around the earth and the earth's orbit around the sun, and in numerous other contexts.

Toward the end of the school year Gordon, who never ate much of his lunch, sat pondering his taco shell and turned to Tim to tell him something he had been thinking about. "Mr. O'Keefe, I think I've discovered something else about infinity."

"Tell me," Tim said.

"Well, if you take your taco chip and break it in half, you could take that half and break it in half, and that half in half, and half and half. You know, infinity times."

"Do you feel like sharing that thought with the class?" Tim asked, smiling.

"Sure."

When we returned from lunch, Tim retrieved his miniature tape recorder and started the recording.

Gordon began, "What I thought when I was eating was that you could cut the taco shell into infinity pieces, just keep on cutting it because you couldn't cut it into nothing."

Tim answered, "He was using the ideas of fractions and infinity. Maybe you could draw a picture and show what you mean."

Gordon drew a semicircle on the chalkboard. "You could keep cutting it and cutting it until it got to be microscopic and after you cut that, then you would cut those pieces into different pieces and those pieces . . ."

Andy jumped in with, "You could use the electron microscope to see it."

Tim reacted by looking to the original author of this idea, "Jonathan, what do you think about this idea?"

Jonathan responded, "It will disappear."

Tim asked, "It will just disappear and just be nothing? Laura, what do you think?"

Laura had been anxiously waiting for a turn to share. She said, "If you used an electron microscope you would probably be able to see little pieces of it."

Gordon added, "It would get past microscopic and you couldn't even see it with a microscope. You could just keep on cutting it even if you couldn't see it."

Tim hypothesized, "Say it was this big under the electron microscope (draws a shape on the board), and just say you could cut that in half. Then you could cut that in half and that in half. Gordon is saying that you could keep on cutting it an infinite number of times."

Abby made another mathematical connection, saying, "It's also symmetrical."

Tim smiled. "So you are thinking of symmetry, fractions, and infinity."

Gordon took the floor again, saying, "You could keep folding it in half."

Andy said, "It would be hard to make it so it could go past the electron microscope because it can go over a million times."

Kyle offered a new perspective: "Well, nobody could cut a taco chip into infinity pieces 'cause infinity . . . it's, it's, to me it's not a number."

Tim was intrigued. He attempted to clarify and connect Kyle and Gordon's ideas. "I see what you mean. It's hard to understand. It's something that goes on forever and none of us could ever experience that. I think that part of Gordon's point is, Gordon, correct me if I'm wrong, it's not so much that a person could keep chopping forever, but that there are pieces that keep getting smaller and smaller and that you could never get to nothing."

Gordon confirmed his teacher's explanation. "Yeah. You would also have stuff left over plus you'd still have a teeny piece left over from what you were cutting."

Tim said, "So no matter how much you cut you would always have something left."

Jonathan joined in again. "There would be something left. I can tell you that but you can't keep cutting it in half. It would get so small you can't even see it. So you'd keep on chopping the table."

Tim asked, "Do you think it's possible to . . . let's pretend that you had a microscope that you could see things as they got smaller and smaller. Do you think that there is an end to things?"

Andy continued, "If you keep cutting it and cutting it, you could keep going up higher and higher on the microscope but it would be hard to keep cutting it because you couldn't see it after a certain amount of chops, like a thousand chops."

Tim ventured, "You have a good point. But is there an end?"

Jonathan answered, "Here's why I think it would turn into nothing because, like, you're biting little pieces off a chocolate chip cookie and they get smaller and smaller until it disappears."

Tim said, "So you think that it would end up disappearing. That there would be nothing left."

Jonathan continued, "When it gets so small, and so small, and so small, it turns into nothing."

Gordon said, "Well, see, what Jonathan said is a crumb would just go into nothing. Well people think it could go into nothing but there's probably still teeny particles left that could easily just be blown away or vacuumed up or something. That's maybe why they think it disappears. Plus you can't see 'em. It's not like you have microscope eyes that you can see every little crumb."

Tim added, "You make some really good points. For one thing, there are things that exist that people don't know about. We can only see so small with a microscope but that doesn't mean that there aren't things smaller than what we can see. People don't know everything."

Curtisha joined the conversation saying, "If you keep cutting it infinity times it would just be a little tiny dot."

Tim responded, "Yes, but Gordon says, in theory, you could cut that dot in half, and cut that dot in half and it could just keep getting smaller and smaller. Gordon thinks you go on forever."

Curtisha continued, "Only 'till it disappears."

Becky questioned, "If it was just a small little speck, how could you get a knife skinny enough?"

Tim said, "You're right. But is there something beyond the point of very little? Let's just pretend that you could cut it in half, and you could cut that in half. Could you keep going forever or would you finally get down to nothing?"

Becky responded, "Sort of . . . I sort of think yes and I sort of think no."

Gordon chimed in, "Curtisha says you could cut it into nothing. If you cut it into nothing . . . It was something at first and then you kept on cutting it. If you could cut it into nothing then you couldn't put the pieces back together. Eventually you could. You'd still have little pieces left. It's not like if you cut it and it disappeared."

Kyle said, "This kind of reminds me of what Dave said about ABC. If you wanted to get to point C you'd still have to go half way. Then you're half way there but you'd still have to go half way. Then you'd have to go half way and half way. Some people say you'd never get there."

Tim inquired, "Would you ever get there?"

Kyle answered enthusiastically, "Yes!"

Laura concluded by suggesting, "I think both ways. Some things would probably get down to nothing and some things you would probably have little pieces left of it."

Reflections

These children were debating, quite articulately, the properties of infinity and matter. The spirited exchange between the children in this group shows us how excited they can be when given the opportunity to muse aloud, knowing that their responses are neither right nor wrong. These authors began to realize that theory is relative and knowledge is constructed through exploration.

On the very last day of school, Tim asked the children to write and draw one final piece about infinity. Kyle started us off in the discussion with a song he'd heard on *Sesame Street* that asks, which came first, the chicken or the egg?

Gordon wrote, "Infinity inches and infinity feet are the same length. But, three inches and three feet are not" (Figure 6–5). He was imagining that, in the land of the infinite, all inequalities in length would disappear. Feet and inches would become the same as they stretch out together in a never-ending manner.

As he read his final piece to the group he must have seen the admiration in Tim's eyes and anticipated his question because he followed up with, "Yes, Mr. O'Keefe, I thought of it by myself!" His teacher smiled in response, marveling at Gordon's ability to reach beyond the physical realm, just as theoreticians developing new strands of mathematics do.

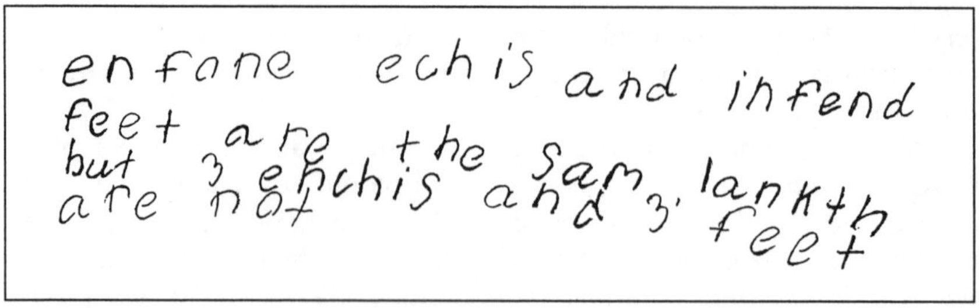

FIGURE 6–5

As teacher-researchers, we learned that the study of infinity revealed a great deal about the learning process in general, our role as teachers, and the concept itself. We learned that concepts cut across contexts; concepts act as lenses that literally change how we view the world; and that concepts connect to other concepts quite naturally (i.e., symmetry and infinity). We learned that children are capable of extremely sophisticated theoretical thinking. Like all good learning, we were reminded that conceptual understanding must be tied to familiar situations. In other words, the infinity study helped us uncover the value of children functioning simultaneously as teachers and learners. The insights they constructed and shared with each other were infinitely more powerful than those we could have discovered on our own.

Table 6–1   Exploring Infinity Over Time

Demonstrations of Authorship	Classroom Context	Mathematical Concept	Strategies for Understanding
Authors reflect and revise by entertaining other possibilities.	Playing subtraction game with Unifix cubes and dice	Infinity, probability	Reclassifying numbers (only zeros)
Authors share their texts with others.	Reading literature books about infinity	Time, shape, spatial relations, length, life cycle, and infinity as a closed loop	Calculating length, quantity
Authors reflect and revise.	Playing class board game	Infinity, length	Counting spaces
Authors express what they know in multiple ways.	Drawing a mural	Life cycle, ecological balance, recycling, energy, and infinity	Counting, using deductive logic
Authors share their texts with others.	Discussion over lunch about teaching	Infinity, time	Using deductive logic
Authors use alternative communication systems.	Singing "This Old Man"	Infinity as a closed loop	Using deductive logic
Authors use alternative communication systems.	Sharing connections to music from home	Infinity as a closed loop, life cycle	Using deductive logic
Authors use alternative communication systems.	Examining the artwork of book covers	Infinity, spatial relations	Using deductive logic, partitioning
Authors initiate their own investigations.	Examining Pizza Hut 3-D glasses	Infinity, spatial relations	Inferring a sequence
Authors share their texts with others.	Discussing properties of a circle	Infinity, symmetry, area	Partitioning
Authors share their texts with others.	Discussing a taco chip over lunch	Infinity, area	Partitioning, matching
Authors grow through prolonged engagements in the process.	Final written reflections	Time, length, infinity	Using deductive logic

Rethinking Curriculum and Evaluation   7

The study of odd and even numbers was a required topic in Tim's class-room, as it is in most second-grade classrooms in the country. Although the topic may look the same on most of the curriculum guidelines, it may not sound the same in individual classrooms. Jerry Harste has said that it is easier to make a classroom look like a whole language class-room than sound like one, and that is one of the points we are trying to make in this chapter. The difference among classrooms lies not in what you see but in what you hear; and the sounds that you hear (and don't hear) are a reflection of a teacher's belief system about what constitutes good learning. Thus, a checklist for second-grade students that includes odd and even numbers cannot capture the sounds of a classroom: the sound of children questioning the definitions of these numbers, noting their functional use in the events of their daily lives, and posing addi-tional hypotheses to pursue. Nor does a checklist of mathematical skills capture the sound of a teacher drawing out children's descriptions of mathematical ideas, valuing the role of anomalies or surprises, encour-aging revision in thinking, and supporting the development of a skepti-cal attitude toward definitions and theories. These are the sounds that infuse a mathematical community; these are the beliefs that either re-strict or expand the potentials for learning; these are the attitudes that define what's possible and shape the mathematical future and vision of our students.

In this chapter we want to look at how a typical mathematical topic like odd and even numbers can be explored in a more open-ended and interpretive manner. We then want to discuss how this particular per-spective toward learning has implications for evaluation and curricular planning. Tim was required to teach odd and even numbers to his sec-ond-grade students. However, as the school year started we noticed that the children had some familiarity with the topic already and began to use it in a variety of contexts.

Using Odd and Even Numbers in Different Contexts

Tim and the class used a stick calendar to keep track of the date (Chapter 2). As the children made observations about the number for the day they often commented that it was either odd or even. Sometimes they talked about the digits themselves. For *27*, Erica remarked, "The first number is even and the second number is odd." During another discussion a few weeks later Andrew noted, "You can split *52* evenly." Alex extended this observation by saying, "Yeah, it's like symmetry; *52* is a symmetry number." The children had been using the concept of symmetry to describe the geometric designs that they had been constructing out of pattern blocks. Alex cleverly tied together these two concepts of symmetry and equivalence to note the numerical symmetry of even numbers. The strategy of splitting a number in half to determine if it was even was useful for children as they discussed larger numbers later in the year. Some children had learned that numbers having *1, 3, 5, 7,* or *9* for a digit were odd numbers. Although most agreed that *7, 17, 27,* and *37* were odd, they were not sure about *70*. Since *7* was one of its digits, some thought it was probably odd. The children used the bundling sticks from the calendar to act out this problem; they noticed that even though the number of bundles of ten was odd, they could partition the last bundle into two sets of five, thereby splitting it evenly. (3 bundles of ten and 5 ones for each half). Thus, the stick calendar provided a meaningful context for children to test out their current theories about how odd and even numbers work.

Another example of the functional use of odd and even numbers occurred during this early part of the year when the children decided to vote on a name for the class salamander. After a preliminary run-off, two choices remained: Spike and Sally. Alex knew there were twenty people in the class and was concerned that the final vote might be a tie. There were eleven boys and nine girls and Alex was predicting that the "boys would vote for Spike and all the girls would vote for Sally 'cause Spike is a boy's name and Sally is a girl's name." He realized that if one boy "switched" his vote there would be a tie. Anticipating this potential problem, he suggested to David, "You and Heidi and Mr. O'Keefe would have to break the tie. Or just one of you. But *not* two of you because it still might be a tie." (The final vote was seventeen votes for Spike and four votes for Sally, with one teacher voting. Alex's sexist prediction never did come true. In fact, as the year progressed, he realized that he could not label the inquiring voices of his peers in such an easy manner, and he gave up predicting along those gender lines.) Alex's concern about a tie did highlight for the children why juries are composed of an odd number of people. As Andrea explained, "If there is an even number, like six, there could be three people saying he is guilty and three people saying he wasn't guilty." Andrea added that if there were an even number of jurors, "You wouldn't know what to do!" Here again the children saw the functional use of odd and even numbers in an authentic context.

During an animal unit, we read *Animal Numbers* (Kitchen 1987) and found ourselves looking at odd and even numbers again. The book takes a mathematical stance toward animal life by focusing on the number of offspring of various species. We thought about other mathematical slants that we could take on animals, such as weight, longevity, and range. Finally, we decided to categorize animals by the number of legs they had; we brainstormed a list of animals with different numbers of legs and found that almost all animals had an even number: two for humans, four for horses, six for most insects, eight for spiders, and one hundred for centipedes; starfish seemed to be the only exception with five arms. The children offered the following explanations for this phenomenon of even-numbered limbs:

ANTWON: So they can hop or jump, or do anything they have to do.

GORDON: They should have an even number because if they had two on one side and one on the other, there would be one ahead and it would be crooked on one side.

BRITTANY: They couldn't walk straight.

LARRY: They couldn't walk really at all if they had three legs. They would fall down. They would keep trying and fall down.

ALEX: If we had one leg we couldn't balance very well.

ANDREW: If they had three legs they would be limping.

ERICA: They would just keep going around in a circle.

The discussion helped to highlight the functionality of having an even number of limbs. Thus, odd and even numbers became a conceptual framework for viewing the animal world in a new way. The children discussed other contexts as well, such as the odd number of games in the World Series or a tennis match. As Andrea explained, "In tennis the players might score the same amount. They would have the same amount of wins." One of the children also suggested the number of eyelets on shoes and sneakers as an example of even numbers. No one was exactly sure if this statement was true so the children counted their eyelets and found that the number ranged from ten to twenty-eight, but each pair of shoes had an even number. Alex offered a reason for this finding: "If you had an odd number of shoelaces, then you'd have one less hole, and you'd have a longer shoelace, and you could trip."

Since the topic of odd and even numbers was one that we kept highlighting, other examples continued to arise as the year progressed. One day Tim observed that the number of pulls on the cabinets in the classroom was always an even number so that he could open the doors more easily. David then mentioned a toaster: there were two-, four-, and sometimes six-slice toasters. He wondered why toasters only came in even numbers. We discussed that the typical serving size is two slices and that multiples of two seemed a logical way to build larger toasters. The children confirmed this observation by noting that they always were served two pieces of toast when they went to a restaurant. Thus, the concept of a ratio—two slices per person—was naturally embedded in this discussion of odd and even numbers.

The pagination of a book also demonstrated another use of odd and even numbers. Abby and Laura wrote a book together and numbered every page with odd numbers (they did not bother to number the back side of each page with even numbers). Since each chapter of their book was only two pages long, they simply numbered the first page of each chapter. They noticed that they had written only odd numbers and shared this observation with the class. Here again the concept of a ratio, one number assigned for each set of two pages, arose in quite a natural way. The children noted the pagination of a book on another day when Larry and Abby took turns reading aloud a twenty-page story they had written together. Afterwards, Ricky remarked, "Abby read the odd pages and Larry read the even pages." His comment showed the class that the pagination of a book was another context for the alternating sequence of odd and even numbers. This interval of two between two odd numbers or two even numbers arose again when Tim was reading aloud *The Land of Oz* (Baum 1985). The characters in the story faced the puzzle of trying to count by twos and land on seventeen. Several children knew the answer right away and chimed in, "Just go by one, three, five, seven, nine—like that." Tim asked, "Are you still counting by twos?" Andrea explained, "Yeah, you just start with an odd number." Antwon was surprised that the characters in the story took a while to solve the puzzle because "Scarecrow should have figured that out 'cause he got a brain." Here a piece of literature highlights the common interval of two that these two sequences share.

On another occasion Deana and Laura were building a large geometric design with pattern blocks. They had created a large flower-like design with a vertical and horizontal axis of symmetry. At one point they called David over to the rug area where they were working and exclaimed, "Look, we found odd and even numbers again!" When David asked them where they had found them, the following conversation ensued:

DEANA: We started out going around and around, and we did it by color [trying to keep the design symmetrical on both the vertical and horizontal axes]. We ended up with three orange and one diamond shapes. [These were the leftover pieces they couldn't use if they were to continue to make the design symmetrical.]

LAURA: He had an odd number and we could *not* even it out. [Since the design had two axes of symmetry, the children needed four pieces to balance these two axes, but they only had three pieces.]

DAVID: What do you mean that you could not even it out?

LAURA: Well, we couldn't even it out because odd you cannot even out with an odd number. Because odd means, like, if you had three and you try to split it up between two people you'll have one extra.

DAVID: So what do odd and even numbers have to do with symmetry?

DEANA: Well, if you want to try to keep it going in the same pattern, and do it on each side, you have to have an even number.

LAURA: If you fold up [the design] this way it will go over and be the same; and if you fold it up the other way it will go over and be the same.

TIM: This is the largest pattern block design with the fewest leftovers, that's still symmetrical that I've seen so far.

This discussion highlights the importance of having children make explicit the connections between mathematical concepts. Deana noted the numerical equivalent on each side of the pattern and Laura showed the matching that is possible when two sides have identical patterns. It is also important to note here that we as teachers continued to support the children to look for odd and even numbers on a regular basis. In this way children come to view the world from a mathematical perspective, as teachers encourage them to strap on these conceptual lenses and look for mathematical ideas in all that they do.

Odd and even numbers arose again in the context of a story problem that Alex wrote (Figure 7–1) in response to hearing two stories, *The Doorbell Rang* (Hutchins 1986) and *Gator Pie* (Mathews 1995). When David asked him how he could partition 180 arrows between two people, Alex responded, "I was going for the middlest number. At first I thought it was seventy. Then I thought it was eighty. And then I came up with ninety-five,

Alex and Christopher

Robin hood had 100 arowwas. Little John had 80. They wanted to make it equle. So they thought and they had 90.

FIGURE 7-1

and then I came up with ninety." He explained that he had to keep revising his estimate until he found "the middlest number." Alex also said he could solve it another way: "If you split eighty in half that would equal forty. And if you split one hundred in half, that would equal fifty. So you just add fifty plus forty." David responded, "Yes, that's another strategy. It works because you're using even numbers." This mention of even numbers prompted Alex and his friend Chris to conjecture about other numbers. Alex speculated, "Yeah, it wouldn't work with odd numbers like five hundred. But three hundred you could split—150 each." David asked him to explain why five hundred wouldn't work. Alex thought about that number again and realized it can be divided evenly; he explained that he first thought it was odd because it had a 5 in it. He and Chris then went on to discuss other numbers like seventy, arguing that it too was even because it had a zero. Chris provided a rationale for why zero is an even number: "Seventy is even because zero is an even number. It's like this person gets nothing, and this person gets nothing, so it's even. They both don't get anything." Alex argued that zero is even because "it's two numbers away from two." The boys had learned that even numbers had an even number as their last digit (including zero) but couldn't explain why that rule really worked. We used the stick calendar to represent the process so that all the children could better understand the reasons behind the rule they had memorized. The children found that seven bundles of ten could be divided into two piles of three bundles each and the last bundle could be broken in half so each person could receive five additional sticks. They came to see that since ten is even, any multiple of ten would also be even. Thus, Alex's story helped the class examine more closely the reasons behind the rules they were following and gain a more informed understanding of numbers that have a "middlest" number.

Several months later Gordon brought up this idea of a middle again when he drew a picture of the moon and wrote, "There is a middle to everything. A middle is a half, but a half is a thing split in a equal amount." He discussed things that had a "length," as well as things that had weight or were comprised of liquids. The discussion led to another examination of the property of a "middle" and its relationship to odd and even numbers. Gordon held up five fingers to illustrate his point: "Every odd number has a finger in the middle, and an even number [he holds up two fingers] doesn't have a finger in the middle, but it has a space in the middle." Thus, fingers provided another useful model to show the difference between odd and even numbers.

As the preceding examples demonstrate, the children found odd and even numbers operating in a variety of different contexts: from using geometric pieces and discussing the daily stick calendar to counting the legs of animals and analyzing a toaster. Mathematical concepts know no boundaries; they are interdisciplinary by their very nature. When we as teachers focus on concepts we invite children to make these interdisciplinary ties. These connections demonstrate to learners that mathematics is a way of thinking, a way of viewing the world. Also, these classroom examples show that the concept of equivalence (even numbers can be divided into two equivalent amounts), which underlies this topic of odd and even numbers, does not operate in isolation. The children naturally connected it to the concepts of symmetry, ratio, and equivalence. This interconnectedness of concepts naturally emerges as children are supported to view the world in a mathematical way. There needs to be a shift in the field of mathematics from skills in isolation to concepts in contexts.

Challenging the Definition of Odd and Even Numbers

From an authoring perspective, odd and even numbers are not a topic that is covered and forgotten but rather a lens for viewing the world. However, another important aspect of authoring texts is the disposition to question the definitions of mathematical terms and challenge the assumptions upon which they rest. It is this spirit of being skeptical and raising alternative interpretations that is not found on the typical classroom checklist of skills to be covered, but it is one of the most important attitudes we can cultivate in our students. Teachers may not be able to check off this inquisitive spirit on a list, but it's in the air and sets the tone for what is possible. It defines which questions are to be valued, what ideas are to be supported, and what risks are worth running. An example of this spirit of challenge and debate occurred when David began discussing odd and even numbers with the class. He was using a series of one-inch squares to show that he could build two towers of equal height with an even number of squares and that he could not do so with an odd number of squares. However, the children challenged what he was doing from the very beginning. When he held up one square and asked if it was odd or even, Andrew said, "It's odd because you can't split it up." Alex disagreed, "Sometimes you can split it up though, like in half. You could split it up in half if you were talking about fractions." David acknowledged that sometimes people can split up remainders so that each person has an equal share but that fractional parts are not really considered when deciding if a number is odd or even. Andrew then challenged this revised definition by proposing, "But if there was only one person and there was one cookie, that would be like an even number. And three people and three cookies—that could be an even number." This idea of equal partitioning appealed to Antwon, who connected it to two stories we had read to the class, *The Doorbell Rang* (Hutchins 1986) and *Gator Pie* (Matthews 1995). Abby then shared that odd and even numbers only involve two people. However, when the class discussed five, this same issue was raised again. When asked if five was odd or even, Chris responded, "Well, actually, it's not even and it's not odd. Because if you have five people they would each get one." David rephrased the problem by asking, "But if we had five blocks and just two people, would each person get the same number of blocks?" Chris knew now that he had to consider two people sharing five blocks without using fractional parts. Again he proposed an interesting alternative: "Yes, they could get the same amount. If they both used two, then they both figure out what to do with the extra one and they both do that *together*." David admitted that sharing the last block in that way did make it seem fair. However, the class did agree that if the last block had to be given to one of the two people, then those people would have different amounts and five would be considered an odd number. New observations and questions arose when the children discussed the number six. Abby noticed that "Six is even because two people would each get three, but three is an odd number." It seemed surprising to her that an even number would yield an odd number of blocks for each person. Laura found another solution that gave each person an even number of blocks: "If you split it up among three people each person gets two blocks." Kyle recalled an earlier conversation that the class had about odd and even numbers to help explain what Abby had found: "We found this out a long time ago. We found a pattern, if you take two odd numbers, like three [plus] three, it would equal an even number." Erica tests out that idea with five [plus] five and finds it works with those odd numbers as well. Tim then asks if this hypothesis holds true for other pairs of odd numbers.

There are several interesting features about this mathematical conversation. First, the children kept using the important word *if* to play around with the definition of an even number: What if we could split up the remainder into fractional parts? What if we considered more or less than two people when dividing a given set of objects? What if we tried to figure out a fair way to share the remainder? Chris suggested this last alternative because he was most interested in this issue of fairness. It appears that Chris considered the fair distribution of the remainder as a legitimate part of the definition of an even number. Allowing the conversation to travel in these unanticipated directions enables learners to explore these mathematical ideas in their own way. It is this incessant poking, prying, and challenging of ideas that enriches and deepens the collective understanding of these mathematical terms and concepts.

Second, Antwon made the connection between odd and even numbers and two stories that the class had read earlier. His comment highlights the crucial role that story plays in restoring a meaningful context to the teaching and learning of mathematical ideas (Whitin and Wilde 1995). Stories are the conduit for carrying meaning; when learners have a reservoir of stories to draw from they will naturally make these connections across stories, tying together contexts and concepts in unique ways.

Third, Abby demonstrated the importance of sharing anomalies with the class. She was surprised that some even numbers yielded two sets of odd numbers (such as six being partitioned into two sets of three). Other children tried to address this unexpected outcome. Laura revised the problem to include three people, thereby giving each person an even number of blocks. Kyle tried to argue more generally that the sum of any two odd numbers will yield an even number. Thus, because the conversation was open ended and invited children to challenge the definitions of odd and even numbers in their own way, there were more questions than answers that were raised. The conversation highlighted these possible next steps:

1. Is it possible to add any two odd numbers together and always get an even number? Do the odd numbers always have to be the same? What happens when we add different combinations of odd and even numbers?

2. What are different ways that we could divide a set of objects among different sets of people, such as six objects among one person, then two people, then three, and then six. What would we find for different numbers? Is there a pattern to our results?

3. What are different situations in which we could divide a remainder into fractional parts? What do we do with remainders in other situations? (A good book for teachers to share with their students about remainders is *A Remainder of One* by Elinor Pinczes [1995].)

4. What are other ways that we use the terms *odd* and *even* in a colloquial sense? Phrases such as "He's the odd man out" or "I feel like a fifth wheel" highlight the characteristics of these numerical relationships.

We invited the children to explore several of these possible directions. We gave them some one-inch squares and asked them to investigate different combinations of odd and even numbers. Elizabeth found two ways to add to get an even sum by either adding two evens or adding two odds. David challenged her to find two ways to make an odd (using only two addends). She found it interesting that there was only one combination for that situation, which she recorded on her paper (Figure 7–2). Her illustration clearly shows that adding an odd number on top of an even base will yield an odd number every time. Andrew made several interesting insights as well (Figure 7–3). He noticed that two odds made an even and he showed it in two different ways (*1 + 3* and *5 + 5*). He also noticed the congruence of the two shapes he had constructed for *5 + 5* when he remarked, "If I just took this one and turned it around, it would be the same size." He then looked at his drawing for *5 + 5*, saw that one *5* could be divided into *3 + 2*, and wrote the following observation: "I think if we took three numbers, it could equal the same number—odd, even, odd, *5, 3, 2*." He placed other squares together to make a larger square but didn't focus on the odd and even properties of that configuration. Instead, he looked at it in terms of its factors, noting that nine ones and three threes comprised that particular square. His investigation could certainly lead to a more detailed look at the different ways squares and rectangles can be created. Again, allowing children to modify the attributes of a problem in various ways provides the seeds for future investigations. Andrew looked at his two by seven rectangle and remarked, "Fourteen odds is an even." He was considering his representation as fourteen individual units. He used this observation to see that an odd number of odds will yield an odd sum and an even number of odds will yield an even sum.

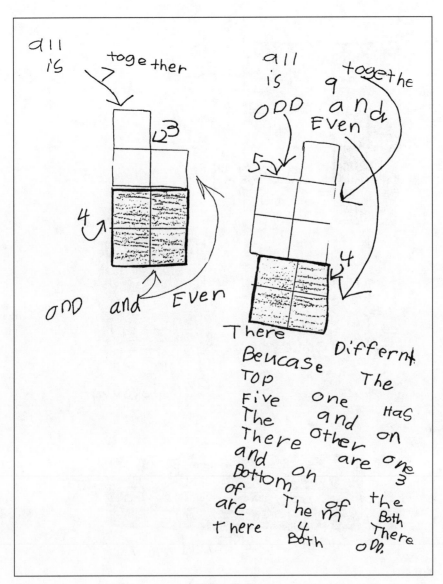

all
is

together
7

23

4

odd and Even

all
is
9
ODD
Even
togethe
and

5

4

There   Differnt
Beucase   The
Top
Five   one   Has
The   and   on
There   other one
and   on   3
Bottom
of   The m of   the
are   Both
There   4   There
        Both   ODD.

FIGURE 7–2

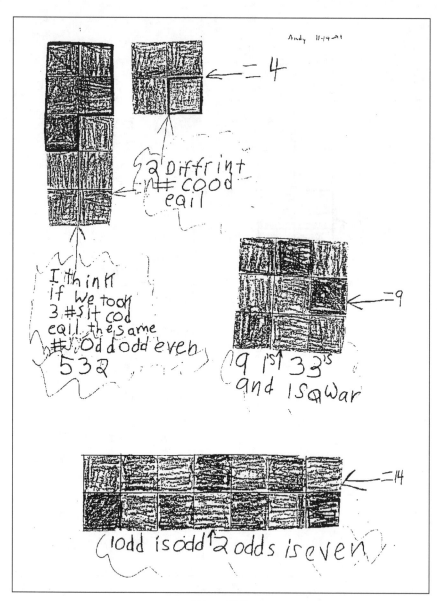

FIGURE 7–3

Taking a Closer Look: Why We Must Strive for What Is Possible

Tim strives to "uncover" the curriculum with the help of his students. He is mindful of the fact that he is responsible for addressing the district objectives and the content in the mathematics textbook. However, he does not let such a requirement stand in the way of doing what is best for children. After taking a close look at the typical "scope" of the curriculum, he realizes that there is still plenty of room for curricular negotiation as long as it is the classroom teacher along with his children who determines how and when the curriculum gets uncovered.

After we reflected upon the diverse ways the children learned about odd and even numbers throughout the year, we realized again that the order in which the objectives and strategies are addressed can be determined by the teacher after careful observation and documentation of the students' needs and interests. When coauthoring the curriculum with the children, teachers encourage them to devise the stories, questions, and personal connections necessary to make the learning their own. Brenda Rogers, a perceptive teacher from Oconee County, South Carolina, said it best: "In attempting to simply cover the curriculum, I realize that we have actually been covering it up." When comparing the depth of the curriculum we have been describing to that contained within the boundaries of the textbook covers, her comment is further illuminated.

The Textbook

If we had limited the conversations and engagements to those predetermined by the textbook (including the enrichment section), the children would have been instructed to do the following:

- Clap odd and even number patterns through nineteen and twenty, respectively.
- Make pairs (of even numbers) on grid paper to twenty.
- Write odd numbers in one color and even numbers in another color to ninety.
- Draw a circle around the odd numbers and a square around the even numbers on a number line to twenty.
- Using odd and even patterns, find the missing numbers on the enrichment page.
- Write odd and even numbers that come between various numbers.

- Use synonyms for *two*, such as *pairs, doubles, twins,* and use these words when talking about even numbers.
- Reteach: Circle the even numbers and draw an *X* over the odd numbers.

  Write *E* for even numbers and *O* for odd numbers.
- Circle *odd* or *even* next to your answer after completing the addition problems on the page. (This assignment occurs twenty pages later in the book.)

The textbook treatment of odd and even numbers is fairly typical of the way topics are introduced to children. The constant testing through exercises, most of which are corrected and returned to students, does not explain how the mathematical idea connects to our lives—why it is important to understand and why it matters.

This is not to say that we should not use textbooks or that they cannot be used effectively. In fact, most teachers are required to use them and we believe they can do so in educationally sound ways. It is *how* we use them that makes the critical difference. When we use them as one of many resources, as a reference that demonstrates possibilities for exploration, textbooks support rather than control the curriculum.

Why We Can't Settle for What Is Typical

We agree with the textbook authors that it is important for children to be able to distinguish between odd and even numbers. We have found that children will do so by questioning the definitions of these numbers, noting their functional use in the events in their daily lives, posing hypotheses, and sharing and revising their ideas about the topic. The textbook focuses on the mere identification of odd and even numbers in a short period of time. However, in Tim's classroom we were fostering an exploratory, inquisitive attitude toward these numbers over a long period of time. It was these long-term, personal investigations that valued children as authors of mathematical ideas.

At a time when there is a groundswell of enthusiasm for a "back to the basics" curriculum, it is as important as ever to strive for what is possible rather than settle for what is typical. As Brenda Rogers put it, "Good enough rarely is." Traditionally, basic skills have counted most in mathematics education. We now understand that we must rethink what counts by focusing on "what matters" instead (Stephens 1990). We have synthesized the differences between the model of instruction advocated in the textbook and the model we have come to value (Table 7–1).

Table 7–1

What Counts	What Matters
Skills in isolation	Concepts in context
Prescriptive directions	Surprise counts
Blind allegiance to the present task	A respect for anomalies to set new directions
Single interpretation of problems	Multiple interpretations of problems
Definitions as unquestioned truths	Definitions as negotiated ideas
A quick overview of topics	A revisiting of concepts over time

Distinguishing Between What Matters and What Counts

What used to count in mathematics were isolated skills, segregated learning, and solitary silence. What matters now are unifying concepts, authoring ideas in authentic contexts, and a focus on strategies for understanding. Concepts unite learners because these big ideas demonstrate that mathematics is a way of thinking. If we are to construct curricula with greater vertical continuity, as some people are advocating (Steen 1990), then the unifying dimension of concepts must be in the forefront of our mind. Concepts are not topics that are covered in a short period of time and then forgotten; rather, they are the broad generalizations that frame how we see the world all the time, in all that we do. This unifying aspect of concepts is beautifully described in a book about symmetry, another important concept in mathematics:

> Human fields of study, especially in modern times, have become increasingly compartmentalized. This is especially true in education. The sciences, the humanities, and the arts have all drifted apart over the years. There has also been an increasing trend toward separation (or specialization) within the scientific world itself: physics, chemistry, biology, etc.
>
> Symmetry, however, can provide a connecting link. It is a unique tool for reuniting seemingly disparate fields of endeavor. Accordingly, symmetry can provide insight into what has been lost in the separations. And considerations of harmony and proportion further help us to

relate things that at first glance may appear to have no common ground at all.

The bridging ability of the symmetry concept is a powerful tool—it provides a perspective from which we can see our world as an integrated whole. (Hargatti and Hargatti 1994, p. xv)

Concepts carry with them contexts for learning. For instance, we see ratio in a miniature doll as well as an architect's model for a bridge; symmetry in the wings of a butterfly and in the painting of Leonardo da Vinci; or infinity on a musical scale and on a class board game. These are the ties that integrate learning. Authors are always focusing on concepts because these concepts form the heart of mathematical thinking. Authors are also meaning makers who use various strategies for understanding the mathematical concepts that help us frame and interpret our world.

As we create curriculum based upon an understanding of what matters, we do so by remembering what we now know about how children learn:

- When we look at learning from a process perspective, we remember to value how children think by giving them time to share their learning strategies.
- When we consider the functionality of mathematical learning, we remember to provide demonstrations for learners so that they come to understand the real purposes of mathematics.
- When we value sense over symbol, we remember to focus on the intentions of learners as they construct and share meaning.
- When we access alternative communication systems, we provide learners with continual opportunities to represent their ideas through different communication systems.
- When we look at the social nature of learning, we provide learners time to converse, share, and learn with others.
- Finally, when we value the role of authoring in learning mathematics, we provide opportunities for children to write about what they know; to share their texts with others; to use multiple forms of communication in concert to reflect and extend meaning; to initiate their own investigations; to have the luxury of sufficient time to grow through prolonged engagements; and to reflect and revise.

Rethinking Curriculum and Evaluation

Such meaningful shifts in curriculum have pushed us to recognize what is possible. But these new insights have also challenged us to pose new questions. We are now questioning current evaluation procedures in mathematics education. Prevalent models do not capture the essence of our children's learning experiences and do not provide the information we need to make informed instructional decisions. We feel an urgent need for evaluation procedures that are theoretically consistent with our model of curriculum. Without a formal device that is compatible with our curricular assumptions, as holistic teachers we are often forced to resort to procedures that were developed for different instructional models and typically serve different purposes. For instance, the exercises in the textbook were to be evaluated in terms of correct responses or accuracy. On the other hand, essential understandings about mathematics and the ways in which children become authors of mathematical ideas are much more complex, exciting, sophisticated, and interwoven. Vygotsky reflects our intentions by suggesting that we study things in motion rather than fossilized behavior (1978). Therefore, we have created an evaluation device that is sensitive to and reflective of mathematical authorship, the various classroom contexts in which mathematical growth occurs, the range and depth of mathematical concepts, and the strategies used for understanding.

In creating the device, we were striving for a framework that would simultaneously capture and promote growth. As Eisner (1985) suggests, evaluation procedures, if they are to be instrumental in the achievement of complex educational goals, need to be useful for determining more than whether simple goals were achieved. Knowing that there have been gains in reading, writing, or mathematics without knowing about the processes that led to those gains tells us little. Outcomes don't tell us much. We need to know how they played the game.

We have found Goodman's notion of "kidwatching" (1982) useful as our new instructional decisions grow directly from looking closely at the children with whom we share our professional lives. In fact, Tim has described kidwatching as the central feature and driving force in his curriculum.

> Kidwatching is a continuous, systematic look at the process of how students learn. It is taking what we know about students and turning that knowledge into effective instructional invitations. It is reporting to students and parents about authentic learning. It is valuing the contributions each child makes within the learning community that is our classroom. It is helping the children realize who is an expert and who they can turn to when they need assistance. It is giving voice to students who might otherwise be silent. It is getting to know each child in as many contexts as possible, to know each child as a person unique in all the world. It is the fuel for our desire to know more about the learning process as well as the continuous refinement of our craft as

teachers. Kidwatching is not something apart from the curriculum but rather it is what holds [the curriculum] together and pushes it forward into new and often unexplored territory. (O'Keefe 1995)

While we have found pure kidwatching without any formal structure quite revealing, we have also felt the need to channel or fine tune our observations to make effective use of them when planning and sharing our insights with the children and their parents. In other words, we have envisioned a framework that would require intentional and systematic kidwatching, would be focused and efficient but open ended enough to capture the nature of the curriculum, and would provide specific information about the growth of the individual children.

Evaluating Mathematical Literacy

The charts we used to synthesize each chapter in this book reflect our current work in evaluation. This evaluation strategy highlights the fundamental aspects of a curriculum that supports mathematical authorship. It can also be adapted to analyze individual children's growth over time, specific mathematical concepts, and strategies for understanding as well as the depth and range of mathematical learning events experienced throughout the day or curriculum.

The stories and strategies that brought the study of odd and even numbers to life in Tim's classroom can also be interpreted and shared efficiently through this device (Table 7–2). While the instrument lacks the rich detail embedded in the stories, it offers another important perspective.

This chart provides a principled structure to analyze the children's exploration and understanding of odd and even numbers. Imagine how much more information we have to evaluate the curriculum and to explain the curriculum to parents than could be ascertained from analyzing correct and incorrect responses on the textbook worksheets.

This model of evaluation requires thoughtful observations on our part but is free enough to capture specifics. It also demands that we attend to context, concepts, and strategies simultaneously. We cannot privilege one over another as they are all interwoven features of the meaning making process (Figure 7–4).

Evaluating Children's Growth over Time

This model can also be adapted to provide portraits of individual children's growth over time. When reviewing individual children's profiles,

Table 7–2   Looking at Odd and Even Numbers Across Time

Demonstrations of Authorship	Classroom Context	Mathematical Concept	Strategies for Understanding
Authors use a variety of materials to generate new ideas.	Using pattern blocks	Symmetry	Finding a pattern, matching
Authors share their thinking with others.	Discussing stick calendar	Equivalence	Partitioning
Authors share their thinking with others.	Voting for a name for class salamander	Equivalence	Predicting, counting
Authors write about what they know.	Sharing a story with the class	Equivalence	Noting alternating patterns
Authors write about what they know.	Numbering pages of a story	Number, ratio	Counting
Authors share their thinking with others.	Reading aloud *Land of Oz*	Number	Counting
Authors grow through prolonged engagements.	Discussing toasters	Ratio	Counting
Authors grow through prolonged engagements.	Studying animals	Equivalence	Matching
Authors use variety of materials to express what they know.	Using squares to show numbers area	Congruence, symmetry	Matching, partitioning

significant patterns emerge that reveal important information about them as authors of mathematical ideas (Figures 7-5 and 7-6).

Aaron, a first grader, consistently initiated his own investigations; used art, mathematics, and writing together; and was comfortable sharing his work publicly. He frequently conducted surveys and composed his own math stories. He learned about quantity, equality, inequality, and equivalence. He used diverse mathematical strategies, such as organizing quantitative data into categories, using the counting-on strategy for addition, using one-to-one correspondence to compare sets, and creating mathematical equations to represent his drawings.

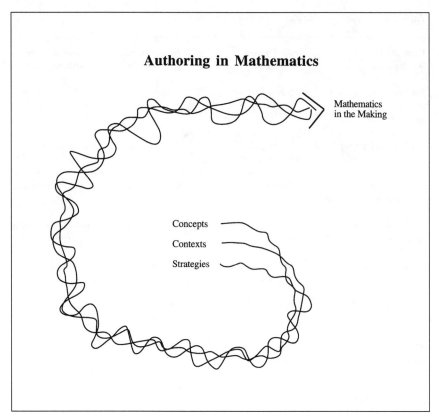

Authoring in Mathematics

Mathematics
in the Making

Concepts

Contexts

Strategies

FIGURE 7–4

Sara, a third grader, consistently shared her mathematical observations with others; she reflected and revised her work to more accurately convey her message; and she used art, mathematics, and writing in concert to construct and convey meaning. She made frequent and important contributions to the group when analyzing class graphs, and she found story a powerful medium to make sense of mathematical skills and concepts and to connect mathematics to her life. She composed stories about frogs, pets, money, and time. She explored a wide variety of concepts through story and the analysis of graphs: sets, variables, relations, ordering, symmetry, progression, equivalence, numeration, and time. She developed an extensive repertoire of strategies for understanding mathematical concepts. Sara used classification, deductive logic, and personal connections with familiar texts when authoring in mathematics.

Evaluating Mathematics
Profile of Individual Learners

Child's Name _____

Teacher's Name _____

Date	Demonstrations of Authorship	Classroom Context	Mathematical Concept	Skills	Strategies for Understanding

(Mills, O'Keefe and Whitin, 1996)

FIGURE 7–5

Evaluating Mathematics
Profile of Curriculum

Teacher's Name _____

Grade Level _____

Focus of Inquiry: Unit of Study _____, Examination of Mathematical Concept _____,
Range of Mathematical Explorations during one grading period _____

Date	Demonstrations of Authorship	Classroom Context	Mathematical Concept	Skills	Strategies for Understanding

(Mills, O'Keefe and Whitin, 1996)

FIGURE 7–6

Putting Skills into Proper Perspective

Throughout this book we have emphasized the value of thinking conceptually, the importance of authentic learning contexts, and strategies for composing mathematical ideas. We have shared stories and strategies that reflect the growth of children in Tim's primary classrooms and lessons we learned from them. We have attempted to push ourselves, and our readers by taking a close look at curriculum and evaluation in one teacher's classroom. While we have learned a great deal from the children and our collaborative efforts, one thing has not yet changed. Tim is still accountable for teaching and evaluating specific skills that are identified as district objectives. We predict that most classroom teachers share this requirement. Therefore, we have included skills in our model, as well as concepts and strategies. By doing so, we hope it will help teachers document their young authors' understanding and use of mathematical operations without compromising the integrity of their curricula. We want teachers to uncover skills within the context of authentic mathematical investigations and document them on the evaluation instrument alongside their corresponding concepts and strategies.

A review of concepts, strategies, and skills is included here to clarify the distinction among these categories and to highlight the unique contributions they all make to the development of mathematical literacy. When we look at skills as the operations or tools that help authors construct and share mathematical ideas, we put them into proper perspective and help children recognize their relative value. Skills are no longer considered ends in themselves but valuable tools for problem posing and solving. For instance, when Aaron initiated and composed his own apple stories, he used subtraction to illustrate what happened to the apples when they fell off the tree. Within the subtraction scenario, he divided

Table 7–3

Demonstrations of Authorship	Classroom Context	Mathematical Concept	Skills	Strategies for Understanding
Authors initiate their own investigations, share texts with others, and use alternative communication systems.	Apple stories.	Equivalence.	Subtraction.	Using art to "show" meaning of equation.

the apples into two sets, healthy and rotten. Therefore, when adding skills to our evaluation device, we would document his understanding and successful use of subtraction.

In Figures 7–5 and 7–6, we have included frameworks for evaluating individual children as well as the curriculum. We believe they help us learn to see what's there as we take a close look at our children. We also believe they help us see new possibilities for curriculum development when we uncover significant gaps in the framework. New invitations and demonstration lessons naturally emerge from such observations. Instructional decisions then grow out of intentional and systematic kid-watching. The evaluation framework helps us do so in an efficient yet thorough way. Although the frameworks currently suits our needs, we are confident we will revise them, as revision is a natural part of growth. We invite you to use them or adapt them to best meet your needs.

A Final Story: Rethinking What Matters and What Counts

After the school year was half over and the children had explored odd and even numbers in these various ways, David had a lengthy discussion with Gordon about some candy. Gordon explained his story in this way: "I was outside and I had five mints. I gave my friend two and I had two. The last mint, I dug a hole in the ground and buried it, so it would be even. I opened out the wrapper and buried it so he [his friend] couldn't dig the hole back and eat it. I dug it down and dropped it in, and buried it back." He explained that they couldn't divide the last mint because it was a hard mint and it would shatter if anyone tried to split it. When David asked, "How many more mints would you have needed?" Gordon answered, "You would need six for three people to have two." David wanted him to explore this idea of divisibility further and so asked the broader question, "When you divide things, why does it work out evenly sometimes and not other times?" Gordon proposes several ideas: "Sometimes, if you have, like, three pieces of bread and two people, you could just cut the other in half, 'cause it's not solid. Or what I could have done is bought more mints at the store, another mint so there'd be enough for three people. But then, if there was anybody else there, I would have to go back to the store and buy a whole bag." Gordon was already changing the variables of the original problem by imagining a different set of people and a different number of mints. David wanted him to continue to play around with these changes and so asked him what he would do if he really did have more mints. Gordon responded, "I could divide it up, but if I had an odd number of mints I might have to bury lots more." He was predicting that with two people and a large number of mints, there would be many more mints left over to bury. Together they discussed the odd numbers seven through fifteen and found that in each case there was always one mint left over.

David commented, "I thought it was interesting that with three we bury one. And even with a number much bigger than three we still bury one." David was trying to have Gordon confront his earlier hypothesis that larger numbers would yield larger remainders.

Gordon took up the challenge and began to imagine other possible numbers: "I bet if it was . . . oh . . . 130, we'd still have to bury just one. No, I mean 140 . . . no, how about 150? That means you have to bury ten . . . cause fifty is an odd number . . . and you can't divide five tens. You would have to bury ten of them." When David asked, "You mean fifty pieces of candy?" Gordon began to reflect on the problem in another way: "Yeah, 'cause how can you divide them. . . . You could put five on that side and five on the other side. See, I was thinking if it was fifty, you would have to bury ten. But you could really just give five to the other person and keep five yourself." He then imagined twenty-five pieces of candy and calculated that each person would get twelve with one left over. The context of candy helped Gordon think about the divisibility of these numbers from another perspective.

As Gordon and David discussed these findings together, they generated still further areas for exploration. The remaining part of the conversation unfolded in this way:

DAVID: So even with this number [twenty-five], you bury one. So even though the numbers are getting larger, you still bury one. That seems interesting to me. It seems like, with the numbers getting larger you maybe ought to be burying more. But you keep burying one all the time.

GORDON: Yeah. Like when you have five you bury one. When you have six you bury two; when you have seven you bury three; when you have eight you bury four. That's how you might be thinking it's going to go. Didn't you think it was going to be like that? [He was more convinced now that there would always be a remainder of one but he was proposing here a pattern of increased remainders as a plausible prediction for what might have occurred.]

DAVID: Like keep adding one?

GORDON: Yeah, let's see what we come up with. Bury five, take away one. Bury six, take away two. That's four. That's it! See, if we always take away [bury] one more we'll always have four [to split between two people]. Bury seven, take away three . . . four. You always get four.

DAVID: Now another thing that we had talked about was that this was all based on two people. Now if there were three people . . . [David tries to have Gordon consider another idea that had been raised earlier, i.e., the result of partitioning objects among three people, not two, but Gordon ignores the invitation and looks to explore another pattern.]

GORDON: Oh, I see what we could do. This is sort of hard to explain. See, four plus four plus four is twelve. That's an even number, hmmmm . . . but three is odd [the set of three fours is odd]. That's odd and it still comes up to an even number. Let's try two [fours]. Yeah, two fours are eight. Let's try four fours . . . sixteen. That's even too. We keep on getting even numbers. Let's try five of them . . . even number again. I think we're getting something here.

DAVID: So what have you discovered?

GORDON: I think with an even or an odd number, with fours, it will still become an even number.

DAVID: Is there anything else you discovered?

GORDON: I think if we put any odd number plus any odd number, and any even number plus any even number, it would still equal even. See, seven plus seven is fourteen—that's even. Put odd plus odd, five plus five is ten—that's even. As long as you put odd number and the same odd number, like seven plus seven, but if you put seven plus eight it wouldn't be even.

There are several important characteristics of this conversation. First, there is the generative nature of the discussion, as Gordon hypothesized about a greater number of mints as well as explored the results of adding an even number of evens and an odd number of odds. Second, Gordon demonstrates the qualities of an inquirer as he runs some risks ("Yeah, let's see what we come up with . . ."), evaluates his efforts in process ("I think we're getting something here . . ."), suggests alternative courses of action ("Or what I could have done is . . ."), makes predictions ("I bet if it was . . ."), revises his thinking ("See, I was thinking if it was fifty . . . but you could really just . . ."), and tests out his hypotheses in multiple ways ("Let's try two. . . . Let's try four fours. . . . Let's try five of them."). The hypotheses he developed opened new questions to explore: (1) Why do larger numbers not yield larger remainders when dividing a set of objects between two people? (2) If five is odd, why are fifty and 150 not odd? (3) Why does an *odd* number of evens yield an even sum? Open-ended conversations that focus on describing, wondering, and hypothesizing forge new mathematical trails to explore.

Remembering What Matters

It matters a great deal that Gordon was provided rich opportunities to compose his own story of learning about odd and even numbers. However, it is important to remember that Gordon is not alone. He lives in a classroom community that nurtures this kind of thinking. His conversation illuminates critical features of mathematical authorship that permeate the class as a whole:

- As authors of mathematical ideas, we see more because we express our understandings in many different ways.
- As authors of mathematical ideas, we question more because we are accustomed to entertaining the alternative perspectives of others.
- As authors of mathematical ideas, we take more risks because we know revision is a valued part of the process.
- As authors of mathematical ideas, we develop more strategies for solving problems because we are respected as sense-makers. In short, we grow more because, for us, mathematics is always in the making.

In the past, we have focused solely on what counts in education. Gordon and his young colleagues remind us how essential it is to revise our traditional notions of curriculum and evaluation. When doing so, we recognize, that *what matters* is really *what counts*.

Epilogue
Reflections from the Teacher: Putting It All Together

Timothy O'Keefe

In this chapter, I have the luxury of writing in the first person about my classroom and the students in my charge. I discuss strategies I use to get started in the fall, mathematical rituals and routines, and the kinds of things we do day to day to maintain an atmosphere of mathematical literacy. In addition, I will share how I introduce strategies for mathematical investigations and discuss how the children and I keep such routines fresh and generative. I will also address how I meet and extend district requirements and how I collaborate with my children's parents. Many of the ideas have already been discussed in detail throughout this book. I will try to refrain from going deeply into activities discussed elsewhere but instead discuss them from a "practical behind the scenes perspective."

Getting Started: Establishing a Tone for Mathematical Learning

An important aspect of my job as a classroom teacher is to convey the idea that mathematics is all around us if we look at the world in this way. In our lives outside of school we use mathematics in keeping appointments (time), figuring out the mileage for our cars (the operations of subtraction and division), baking and cooking (measurement, fractions, ratios), making purchases at the grocery store (estimation, subtraction), and keeping a checkbook balance (addition, subtraction). Children should realize that mathematics is deeply rooted in the daily routines of people's lives and that it extends far beyond the content of the mathematics textbook during math period.

We can bring mathematical concepts, strategies, and skills into full view of students by making it a part of our regular, daily life in the classroom. When we begin the day with a mental math activity or open up opportunities for children to discuss mathematical questions and insights by using a math journal, children begin to feel comfortable thinking like mathematicians.

Mathematical Rituals

I will explain some of our most common and successful classroom rituals. These are not intended to be taken and used as they are presented but as examples that may be helpful to teachers in coming up with their own rituals that capitalize on the circumstances and children's needs and interests in their own classrooms.

Timing the Lunch Count

When I was teaching second grade, one student timed the class as we recorded our lunch count. Michael wasn't asked to, but he had a fancy timer on his new wristwatch and felt compelled to do so. The children were intrigued with his finding and became determined to improve the current rate at which daily classroom routines were conducted. Thus, timing the lunch count became a ritual. The record was posted, semipermanently, on the chalkboard until it was beaten and replaced. I purchased a digital stopwatch that could time events to hundredths of a second. This was hung on a low hook so that any time it was needed it was accessible. Soon after we started timing the lunch count everyone wanted to try their hand at the stopwatch. So we formalized it by rotating around the class alphabetically. From the very beginning of the school year, on a daily basis, we were using and discussing decimals to represent a short amount of time (usually less than twenty seconds) and comparing decimals to see how close we had come to our record. A few children each day used scrap paper to figure out the difference between our daily time and the record. What may on the surface appear to be a mundane exercise was a very serious matter for the class, which became confident in using decimals and had a clearer understanding of the measurement of time.

I had the privilege of being promoted with the class and so, in third grade, I was working with many of the same students. Consequently, we built upon and extended our daily time/decimal ritual somewhat. We timed the attendance count and the timer's job each day was to write the time on the board along with the record. Every student was asked to think of the difference between the two times and raise their hands when ready with an answer. Some days this would be easy if regrouping was not involved. Other days the children had to really study the problem, particularly if the subtraction involved regrouping across zeros. For example:

$$
\begin{array}{r}
12.04 \\
- \underline{11.86}
\end{array}
\begin{array}{l}
\text{Today's Time} \\
\text{Record}
\end{array}
$$

When everyone thought they had the answer, one person was chosen to say what the difference was. Our method of choosing a person to answer was pulling a name from the "random cup." Everyone had their name on a slip of paper placed into the ritual cup—a large coffee mug. Whenever a name needed to be selected at random (and these occasions became very frequent after the introduction of the name cup), the cup was called into play. This was deemed a fair way to choose since everyone had an equal chance of being selected.

Most often, if the person selected made some mistake in their mental computation, others might suggest, "Oh, I know what he did," or "You almost had it." What could have been a big risk for error became an exercise in camaraderie. This was also an excellent time for strategy sharing of shortcuts for these types of problems. We also looked at the difference as a fraction and determined if it could be reduced. If the difference was .12, for instance, it was rewritten as $^{12}/_{100}$. The children quickly learned that if the numerator and denominator are both even numbers, then the fraction could be reduced. After demonstrating this strategy of reducing fractions to the class several times at the beginning of the year, it was added to the routine.

This daily activity, which grew out of the children's interests, took only about three minutes each day; it was an exercise in mental computation involving subtraction of decimals; the children were often regrouping from the first week of school all the way until the end of the year. As authors of mathematical ideas they set challenges for themselves that stretched their thinking as mathematicians, promoted collaboration, and made effective use of our class time. The children knew that they were respected as authors for these group and individual endeavors.

Extending Calendar Time Rituals

The calendar was used in different ways across classes as part of our daily ritual. The "stick calendar" or "cube calendar" (using base-ten blocks) has already been mentioned in Chapters 2 and 4. This strategy invited children to generate mathematical names for a number.

The calendar was used in other ways as well. Open-ended calendar questions were generated during our opening activities. Examples of these in the transition first-grade classroom are provided in Chapter 2.

When I was teaching second grade, we created a money calendar. Five plastic bags were tacked onto the cork strip above our chalkboard. These were clearly labeled "penny," "nickel," "dime," "quarter," "dollar." Each day of the school year, a penny was added to the proper bag and any exchanging of coins was completed so that the fewest number of coins were used to represent each day. On day seventy-five, for example, we would have to change the two quarters, two dimes, and four pennies, of day seventy-four, to three quarters. After completing the exchange, the class would count the entire amount together starting with the largest denominations and moving to the smallest. I found this particular ritual to be very helpful in that we had some predictable, daily practice with counting money. Just as children learn to talk by listening and engaging in meaningful conversations on a daily basis, so too my children learned about the quantitative nature of money and the relationship between various denominations through natural opportunities to talk about them during the daily calendar ritual.

Initiating and Maintaining Graphs and Surveys

Another important daily ritual involved graphs and surveys. Although they have been discussed throughout the book it is important to note practical details involved in their implementation. I encouraged individuals to pursue answers to their questions by giving them clipboards and asking them to determine a question and ask the class. To promote mathematical authorship, I asked the children to make decisions regarding the form of their surveys based on the content or nature of their questions. Individual authors collected, organized, and displayed numerical data in their own ways. They published their findings by displaying the results on large chart paper to share with the class.

I also posed questions and created surveys. Often when the children entered class in the morning, I had a large survey posted near the front with a question for them to respond to. Children would often recommend questions for me to investigate with the class. They suggested queries like, "Do you believe there are aliens in outer space?" or "What kind of pizza is your favorite?"

The debriefing sessions that followed mathematical publishing were very informative. I usually started the discussion with, "What do you notice about the graph?" or "What do we know now that we have this information?" The answers ranged from which column has the most to complex discussions on taste, behavior, styles, current events, literature, or biology. Of course the rich language of mathematics was embedded throughout the discussions. Another important question we made a habit of posing was, "Who would like to know this information?"

A couple of years ago, a curriculum committee I served on got a very large Venn diagram painted on a wall in the cafeteria. The two intersecting circles, each with a diameter of ten feet, were painted with high gloss, enamel paint. Classes could use this any way they liked. We felt that this use of Venn diagrams would be an excellent way to publish large surveys and to include everyone in the school in the process.

At the end of second grade last year my class posed a question for the entire school, "Do you like ketchup, mustard, neither, or both?" We passed out notes to the entire school along with a small Venn diagram on poster paper to each classroom. During the week prior to collecting the notes, we had announcements read over the intercom about the health value of the two condiments, the fact that ketchup can be spelled two ways (*catsup*), and facts about mustard being one of the oldest spices with tremendous variety in the recipes. "Do you want to find out the school's preference? Keep watching the Venn diagram in the cafeteria and don't forget to vote!"

When the day came for us to collect the diagrams from the various grade levels, the children were ecstatic. All of the preferences were sorted, counted, and carried down to the cafeteria for posting on the large diagram. While this project took quite a lot of preparation and time to carry out, most children were intensely serious and businesslike.

After posting the results we came back to the room and generated ideas about who would like to know the information we just gathered. Our answers were written on large chart paper that was mounted on the wall next to the Venn diagram.

"A deli owner would like to know this to have the right stuff out for hot dogs and hamburgers," suggested Sara.

"The cafeteria people would like to know so they can have the right amount of things out too," said Amy, bringing the practical use of this information close to home.

Jim suggested, "The people who make those things would like to know because if a lot more people like ketchup and most people don't like mustard very much, as was found in our survey, then the mustard people should get out of the business!"

A little paint and some note pads made it possible for our class to move beyond our room in answering questions and thinking mathematically about the ideas and opinions of our whole school. Other questions posed for the Venn diagram were, "Do you celebrate Christmas, Hanukkah, neither, or both?" "Do you have brothers, sisters, neither, or both?" and "Do you own a cat, a dog, neither, or both?" Through this project our class became authors of mathematical ideas published throughout the entire school.

The Class Math Journal: Publishing Mathematical Ideas

We have already mentioned numerous ways to publish mathematical ideas: sharing graphs and surveys, math stories, and the stick calendar; creating math games for others to play; developing projects in the newsletter and attendance surveys; and exploring reactions to mathematical literature. In this section, I will feature one strategy that made a significant difference in our general understanding of and attitude toward mathematics.

I had noticed how popular it had been to publish via our public journals. For years we have kept a science journal in the science area to record and share observations about science materials, experiments, and the class pets. For a time, the children were invited to write in *The Good Things Journal* in an effort to help reduce tattling and to encourage children to look for positive behavior to share with the class. Whenever a child composed an entry in one of the class journals, the author was automatically given time to share it at the next class meeting.

When I look back at our recorded entries for the third-grade mathematics journal, I am amazed at the depth and diversity of the entries. Typically when mathematical texts were shared there was a period of discussion about them. The discussion often went far beyond the question or observation and could go on for several minutes.

Jokes and riddles, interesting patterns, math puzzlers, graphs from magazines and newspapers, simple mathematical questions, shortcuts and different ways of performing algorithms, examples from the real world of recent topics of study, mathematical magic tricks (some found in magazines, some taught by friends and parents, and some discovered), mathematical models, and many other ideas made it into the math journal.

I contributed to the math journal regularly to be sure that it remained a viable and respected activity. My additions to the journal included an entry about the amazing amount of mathematics one can read on a cereal box and a mathematical challenge to figure out my gas mileage given odometer readings and the amount of gas consumed.

On the very first page of the journal Jim rewrote a joke he read involving the metric system (Figure E–1).

After paying well in advance for the school yearbook Jeffery included the entry shown in Figure E–2.

Kyle, well known as the best artist in the class, drew some examples of arcs he used for portraits (Figure E–3). Arcs were discussed at great length the same day as his entry.

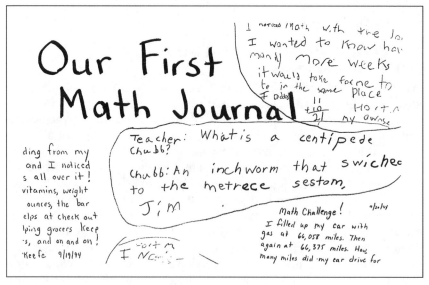

FIGURE E–1

FIGURE E–2

FIGURE E–3

Alex created a visual representation of $^1/_{100}$ of a second (Figure E–4). This was inspired by our time for the lunch count that day of 11.99 seconds. He traced around base ten blocks to create his picture.

Children were clearly authoring mathematical ideas in the math journal and publishing them for a very receptive group. My role in this endeavor was simple: to provide a large blank book (construction paper stapled together) and a place for it in the room. While I also participated by adding entries of my own, I was no more or less in charge of this than anyone else in the room. My biggest contribution was that I gave it time, and that is something that only the classroom teacher can do. In so doing, I found that the discussions and positive feedback among the authors made this a very productive use of our time.

In October Hart taped a chart he had taken from *USA Today* into the math journal (Figure E–5). Hart shared it with the class.

I began by noting, "Hart brought in an interesting article from the newspaper for our math journal."

Hart said, "The state where teachers' pay is the highest is Connecticut, which is rounded to fifty thousand dollars—and that's a lot. South Carolina is the thirty-ninth. It's way down the list."

I asked, "What do the columns tell us?"

Hart answered, "One column tells us the percentage, one tells us the money, and the other tells us the state. The average for all the states is rounded to thirty-six thousand dollars. Some teachers, like Mr. O. for instance, get paid a little extra. Mr. O. probably gets paid a little more and some teachers probably get paid less."

I clarified, "That's based on a few things. One is how long you've been teaching. Next year is my seventeenth year. That's about as high as I can go. Another is how much education you have. What does *average* mean?"

Hart answered confidently, "That's the middlest number you could be. I want someone to guess the lowest state."

Amy chimed in, "I know. I looked. It's South Dakota."

Hart responded, "No, that's the second lowest. The lowest is Mississippi. Guess the second highest."

Tim asked, "Is it Hawaii?"

Hart said, "No, it's Alaska. The third highest is New York. Then it's New Jersey."

Tim made a connection, "All those states are very far north. Let's pull down the map and have a look. The northeast seems to have pretty high teachers' salaries. Let's see what's on the bottom end. Mississippi, that's down in the southeast, close to us. South Dakota, North Dakota—Louisiana is also in the southeast."

Amy added, "It might be that they don't have as many schools as other states."

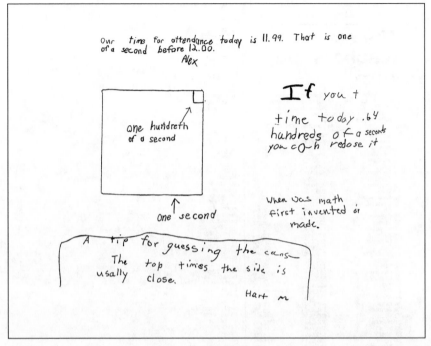

Our time for attendance today is 11.99. That is one of a second before 12.00.
Alex

one hundreth of a second

one second

I f you t time today .64 hundreds of a seconds you can redose it

When was math first invented or made.

A tip for guessing the cans The top times the side is usually close.
Hart M

FIGURE E–4

Tim concluded the conversation by suggesting, "You may be right. In some places it costs more to live than other places. A hundred dollars in New York City probably wouldn't buy you many clothes. Down here in South Carolina you would probably be able to get more things. They would have to make more up there to get the same amount of things."

While Hart did not write the article or compile the data he brought in to share, his analysis and questions made it meaningful for the class and initiated further questions and hypotheses from his peers.

The value of sharing ideas cannot be overstated in a classroom where everyone is respected as valued members of the literacy club of mathematics (Smith 1988). Publishing is an important way for students to have curricular ownership and it demonstrates that everyone in the community is an author with valuable ideas to share.

Including Parents in the Community

Part of creating a community in school is making sure that the people who really matter are connected to the classroom. Obviously the students and teacher make up a big part of that community but it is often

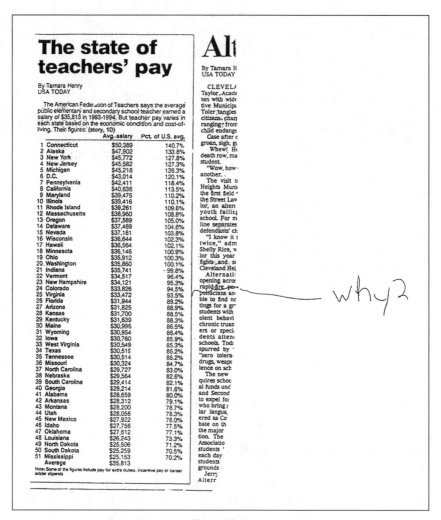

FIGURE E–5

difficult to give parents a voice in what happens in schools. Certainly there are opportunities for parents to be involved through PTAs and advisory councils. Volunteer programs have also been successful in different settings. Yet, I wanted something more. I wanted an explicit way to invite parents into the curriculum—to give them a genuine voice, to truly collaborate with them. My weekly homework projects have enhanced my curriculum in these ways.

While teaching transition first grade, early in the year I sent home a short homework assignment for the children to work on with their parents. The students had illustrated a nursery rhyme and I simply asked the parents to listen while the children read the poem and then wrote a short note to me about what they liked about how their child read. The responses were very positive and I became aware of the potential of asking parents to work with their children at home and then write down observations for me to read.

I decided to formalize the project. It soon became known as the *Homework Newsletter*, which I continued to send home once each week. Chapter 4 provides an example of the newsletter. I will expand on the idea here to explain the logistics and further bring out the potential of this simple but effective strategy.

Many of the ideas for the *Homework Newsletter* projects came from the students themselves. As I was getting my notes together for the news each week I would solicit suggestions for the project from the children. Sometimes the children would ask to repeat an activity they enjoyed in school; these became known as reruns. Other times they would make connections to something we were studying and suggested a project that would correspond with a unit or topic of interest.

The parents' comments about their children's work became a valued source of information for me and contributed to my record keeping. I also found that I could naturally encourage them to teach and learn from one another by publishing their comments, questions, and suggestions into subsequent newsletters. Thus, the *Homework Newsletters* became a forum—a written conversation—among the parents of my students. They coached each other on positive ways to react to children's work and helped each other to learn to see what was inherently valuable in their children's work.

My role focused on preparing the news from the class: what we were studying, materials we could use from home, reporting who might have just had a new brother or sister, introducing new students, and so on. I also wrote about accomplishments of the group and often chatted, informally, about my philosophy of education and how that becomes classroom practice. I answered any questions that came up that I felt everyone should know and moderated parents' conversation by including a section of parents' comments from the previous *Homework Newsletters*.

Many of the activities I asked the children to do with their parents at home were mathematical in nature. Sometimes it was necessary to distribute materials with the *Homework Newsletter* such as rulers, glue sticks, cloth measuring tapes, and graph paper. Among the mathematical invitations were projects about graphing heart rates during different activities, creating a measurement chart of things around the home, graphing the birthdays of friends and family members, and creating math stories about time and money (see Chapter 5).

Early in the year, I began encouraging the parents to frame their comments in the form of three positive observations (pluses) and a wish or a goal for the children to achieve.

Wednesday, October 23, 1991

Dear Parents:

Every week it seems like I'm thanking the same children and their parents for participating so well in the homework/newsletter project. Once again I was pleased to read your comments and the children were proud to report that they had read their books to their folks. The 3+'s and a Wish format for your written feedback seemed to work well. It really makes us focus on the positive things the children are accomplishing instead of emphasizing what they cannot do. The wish then becomes a goal for something we can work on in the future. This also helps us to see children as individuals. Here are some examples of your pluses: "I am pleased that the trip stayed with her and that she was able to write about it"; "Gordon is getting better at reading what he writes"; "Jonathan was very proud of it because he completed it"; "I liked the beginning to end flow of the book"; "He remembers events from early in his life, i.e., having a dog . . . accurate progression of events"; "I loved the humorous angle of Deana's trip to the fair"; "Her first publication will be treasured!" Here are some of your wishes for the youngsters: "I wish the order of events will be chronological next time," "That there was more writing practice so that the neatness would improve," "I wish Larry would write more about his feelings," "He needs to be more detailed," "Working on better sentence structure—not choppy." Your comments are always helpful to me and I think this allows us to see some of the same things happening at home that we see at school.

In class we have been talking a lot about reading lately. Many children see reading as simply sounding out words. To others reading means saying aloud the words on the pages in their readers. Reading is really much more than that as some of the children told me when I asked, "What is reading?" Ricky: "Reading is making the words make sense." Kyle: "Reading is understanding what the author is trying to tell you. Reading is more fun when you understand." Rebecca: "Reading is saying in your mind. Like if you don't know what a word is, you can put a word in that makes sense with the sentence." Jonathan: "You read all the time. Like your gas things and when you buy a telephone. You have to read about how it works." Ashley: "You have to know how to read to get somewhere. You have to be able to read signs and maps. If you don't know how to read you might get wrecked or something." Much of what these children are saying is that reading is meaningful and has a real purpose. I'm sure that you all agree.

Included in this week's newsletter is a handout on what makes language learning easy or very hard. I think this is very connected to what reading is and, to a great extent, what math is. This is written by Ken Goodman who is a leader in education. I'd be interested in your comments on this brief list.

The homework this week has to do with mathematics. We have been making many types of graphs in school from simple picture graphs to complicated opinion surveys. For homework I would like for the children to make one graph with graph paper and another using the same information but showing it a different way. The children first write down the names of family members along the bottom of the graph paper. Then they fill in the bar up to the age of that person. Let's try to have at least three people represented on the graph. Then ask the child to come up with his/her own way to show that information. These should be very diverse and originality is valued for this project. The idea is to get the children used to looking at information in different ways. I hope they find this activity interesting and challenging. Some ideas were discussed in class and you may also help with ideas. Be sure to record some observations for me. You may want to use the 3+'s and a wish format. Thanks again for all that you do in helping with these projects and thanks for reading!

Tim O'Keefe

The previous homework project invited the children to read family stories they had published during writer's workshop. The parents' comments were embedded in this letter to provide demonstrations for each other. Then I initiated another experience to be completed by and reflected upon by the families with whom I work.

Most of the children's work and parents' comments are self explanatory. In Kyle's case, the symbols he chose have personal meaning (Figure E–6). His dad was an avid hunter and was very much interested in guns. The sum of the price tags equals his age. Kyle's mother was very much interested in ecology and her age is represented by worlds. His brother Eric enjoyed fishing and his age is symbolized by a stringer of fish. Mandi, Kyle's little sister, liked playing with dolls, which explains her age symbols. His parents comments are shown in Figure E–7.

Deana's "cake graph" was probably a reflection of the pie graphs created in class (Figure E–8). While fractions of the circle colored in by Deana may not be entirely accurate, she demonstrates a good understanding of the form and function of this type of graph. The entire circle, the result of tracing around a can, represented the sum of the ages of her family members. Her mom and dad were, of course, the oldest, taking up the largest sections of the circle. Deana's father was slightly older than her mother therefore his section is larger. Deana, who was eight, was two years younger than her older sister Carrie. Even without using any formal measurement devices, Deana constructed a graph that is remarkably

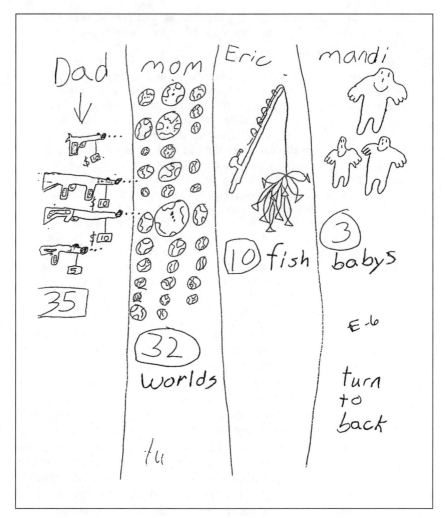

FIGURE E–6

accurate and demonstrates a good understanding of the process. Her mother's comments are shown in Figure E–9.

Traditionally, pie graphs are used to show a total quantity, such as how a student spends her allowance. Some might argue that a bar graph would have been more appropriate for Deana to use because it could have shown the comparison in ages more efficiently. However, I feel that children need opportunities to experiment with various forms of graphs in their own way. My role is to help children note the potentials and limitations of each form of representation and also to encourage them to invent their own.

As parents and their children collaborate in the homework endeav-

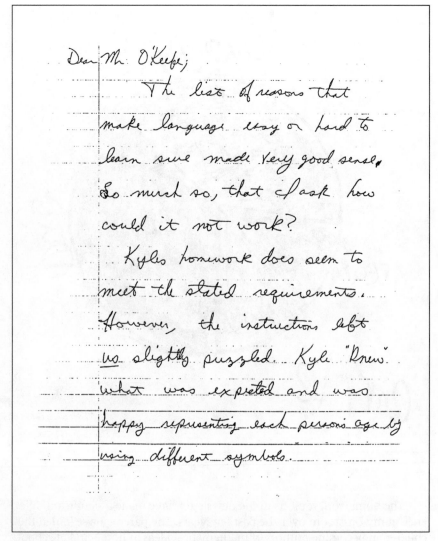

Dear Mr. O'Keefe;

The list of reasons that make language easy or hard to learn sure made very good sense. So much so, that I ask how could it not work?

Kyle's homework does seem to meet the stated requirements. However, the instructions left us slightly puzzled. Kyle "knew" what was expected and was happy representing each person's age by using different symbols.

FIGURE E–7

ors, both parties become authors of mathematical ideas and agents of the curriculum. I would not suggest that all other teachers directly follow my lead and create weekly homework projects. I include it in this section of the book as a demonstration of my desire to elicit greater collaboration with my children's parents and to show how I resolved a critical void in my curriculum. If other teachers are interested in developing a similar parent communication strategy, of course it would have to be modified to suit the individual teacher, classroom, and school.

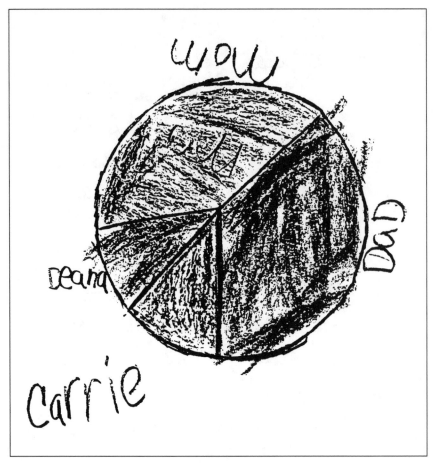

Figure E–8

The homework projects in the newsletter have made a significant difference in my classroom over the past few years. The parents have joined their children in becoming authors of mathematical ideas at home and at school.

Uncovering the Curriculum: It's About Time

When working in a traditional school setting, it became very important for me to know the district expectations for mathematics. These were clearly laid out in our math textbook and the district curriculum guide. The issue of uncovering (versus "covering") the curriculum by using the textbook dominated my planning. Given my beliefs about how children learn best, the choice was obvious. When opportunities arose to capitalize

10-24-91

Deana

+ With a little help from her Dad, Deana easily marked up the bar graph.

+ When questioned about another way to show the same information, Deana quickly came up with the "cake" graph idea. She told me it had been discussed in class.

+ It was Deana's idea to color her "cake."

Wish: That Deana would be more willing to do her homework assignments; i.e., that she would look forward to our weekly challenge instead of dreading it.

Janice L.

FIGURE E–9

on the students' curiosity or interests, I seized them and tried to put them into functional use. In other words, I tried to give a realistic perspective on the use of concepts and operations and relied on the book or scope and sequence chart as little as possible. I will share a unit of study on time that the children and I coauthored to demonstrate how I managed to negotiate curriculum.

Our daily and weekly schedules were posted on a large chart at the front of the room with the times of activities (P.E., music, media center, art), recess, lunch, and the signal bells that indicate the end of the day and the opening of school. When students asked, "How much longer until lunch? I'm getting hungry!" I often responded, "Look at the schedule. What time is lunch? Look at the clock. What time is it now?" These became individual lessons in telling time, but it was clear that there was a need for some explicit group lessons on "telling time." I was aware that telling time on a standard clock to the nearest five minutes was a district objective and that there was a chapter in our mathematics text devoted to time and money. Typically, time and money are taught later in the year because they are difficult for many young ones to understand when they are taught in isolation.

Coincidentally, at the same time, we were noticing recent problems keeping the restrooms clean. This was a particular concern of ours since our door was located just across the hall from both the girls' and boys' restrooms. Hart suggested that we make a chart for boys and girls to sign up on and to indicate the time they left for the restroom and the time they returned. We all agreed that this would be a good idea. If a custodian, teacher, or student discovered a mess they might be able to determine, with the help of the chart, who had been using the restroom around the time the mess was made. Most other classes visited the restrooms en masse, so we determined that we needed a way to be sure no one was abusing the privilege from our room to simply use the restroom when needed. "What time is it?" became the urgent question of the girls and boys standing at the list with legs crossed or while jumping up and down. Knowing how to tell time became important quickly.

Teaching Time Holistically

I decided that I would do my best this year to "teach time" from whole to part or from the underlying concept to the skills and strategies involved. Briefly, we began with the motions of the earth: the orbiting of the sun (creating a year), the tilt of the earth in its orbit creating times when we are closer to or farther from the sun (creating the seasons), and the rotation of the earth on its axis (creating day and night). The earth takes 365 spins or rotations as it travels around the sun. As authors of mathematical ideas, we were focusing on the meaning of the units. The emphasis was on what *makes* a year, not on the numeral itself. We also examined the balance of gravity (which is the force pulling us toward the sun) and centrifugal force (which propels us away from the sun).

While astronomy is *not* typically taught in our district in grade two, this particular discipline was important in understanding the background for telling time on a standard clock. Mathematics is not disconnected from other forms of communication or disciplines in the real world. Therefore, I made concerted efforts to help children understand those natural connections in my classroom. We also looked at methods of telling time throughout history from simply looking at the sun's position in the sky to shadow clocks and sundials to water clocks and to the earliest pendulum clocks with only one hand to represent the hours. From there we explored standard clocks with hour and minute hands and our recently invented digital clocks.

Along the way to reading time on a standard clock, we had many fascinating discussions on the nature of time—past, present, and future. During one of these whole-group discussions Mary had an idea that was so pressing that she asked if she could leave the group to get her ideas on paper. Her model or explanation is seen in Figure E–10.

Mary's explanation began with, "It is like the present never existed." Her model represents the past and future as creatures with many feet because "They change into each other so quickly." Clouds of dust and lines indicating rapid movement also illustrate her point. When asked about the words coming from her mouth in her self-portrait, ("I like your horse") she replied, "*As soon* as you think or say anything it is in the past."

The class recognized the power of authoring through models and was fascinated with the new images Mary's model conveyed. Several of the children followed her lead.

Matthew also had an interesting way to show the relationship among the past, present, and future (Figure E–11). Matthew and his family bowl recreationally, and in his model he drew a bowling ball to represent the future. The triangles represent the present. The parallel lines and arrows indicate pushing from right to left. "The future," he explained, "is rolling. It slides into the present, which turns into the past. And it goes really fast. Instantly!" These pictures of the past, present, and future were helpful visual images that enabled the children to better understand the relationship among these abstract segments of time.

Yes, But Did They Learn How to Tell Time?

This is the kind of question that frequently emerges from discussions with teachers who are skeptical of holistic instruction. They often appreciate the sophistication of children's responses but always retreat to what

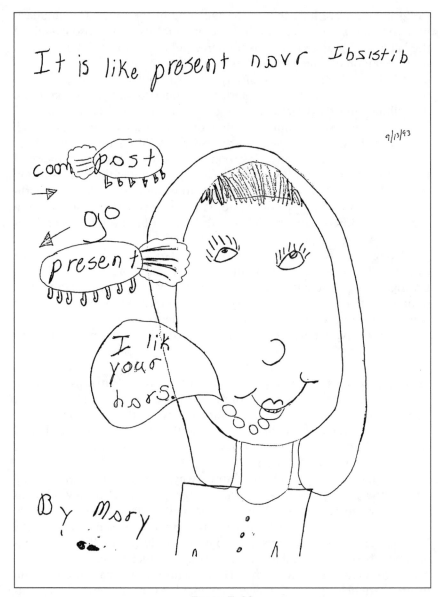

FIGURE E–10

we as educators have determined to be the "bottom line." Did they learn how to tell time? My honest answer is a resounding, "Yes, of course!" In fact, the mechanical aspect of telling time, I think, came more easily to this group of students because of a more thorough analysis of the reasons how history and astronomy connected with it. Less time and effort

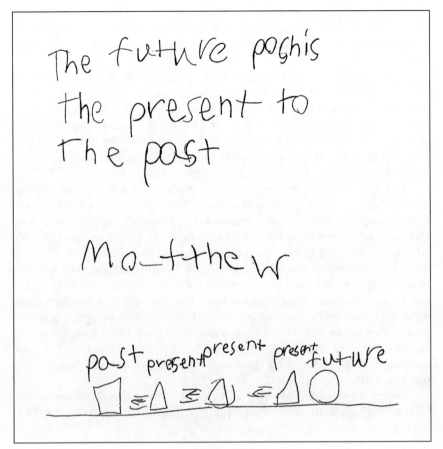

The future poshis
the present to
the past

Matthew

past present present present future

FIGURE E–11

needed to be put into the steps of telling time on a standard clock because the students had a good understanding of the *how* and *why* of telling time.

Generating Curriculum

In October, a parent and I were planning a walking field trip to the Piggly Wiggly grocery store for most of my class. Several of my students were pulled each week for an entire day to participate in the gifted and talented program. Matthew's mom had arranged the trip for this day in an effort to make the rest of the class feel special too. Of course, I agreed with her intentions and predicted that the experience would provide rich mathematical demonstrations and functional engagements as well.

We planned for the children to work in pairs to find all of the items on their grocery lists, estimate the total, and to see how close their predictions were to the actual bill. I met with the store manager the week prior to our trip. As planned, he had everything ready for us when we arrived.

Before beginning our mathematics project he took us on a tour of the store. As we visited each department the children were shown around and given a treat from that particular area. The children received apples from the produce section, cookies from the bakery, meat stickers from the meat department and helium balloons from the florist. The balloons were tethered to the shopping carts on long strings making it easy to locate everyone while we were "shopping."

Our trip went according to plan. Everyone put a great deal of time and thought into the estimation activity. They also experienced the supermarket in a fascinating, unique way. Throughout the tour, they shifted perspectives from consumer to butcher to florist to manager. We all walked into the freezer room and experienced subzero temperatures for a few moments, a very rare feeling in South Carolina. We saw the baker mixing dough and placing small balls into bread pans that would rise to be ten times their original size. We watched the butcher grind meat and package it for display and purchase. The manager explained how they used computerized cash registers to keep inventory, do analysis on items sold, and help reorder food. So many of the benefits from our short field study were immeasurable and went far beyond my planned estimation project.

When we returned to class with our little treasures, I wanted to debrief and reflect with some guided practice on estimation. At least, that is what I had written in my lesson plans.

Rethinking My Curricular Estimation

The helium balloons became very distracting. I had asked the students to tie them to their chairs and to take them home at the end of the day. The children couldn't keep their eyes and hands off of them. It was getting a little irritating.

Finally, after tugging on her balloon string for a while, Michelle asked, "I wonder what my balloon will pick up?"

"What do you mean?" I responded.

"What sort of things would my balloon hold up if I tied it on?"

"How could you find out?" I said, resigning myself to the fact that we would probably have to return to my lesson on estimation at some later time.

"We could just tie stuff on and see if it floats up," explained Corina as she pulled on her balloon string.

"How could we show what we find?" I could see where this was going.

"Make a chart!" said two or three children in unison.

"OK, OK, but be systematic," I said, giving in to the inevitable. Almost before I finished, many children began to untie their balloons and collect paper and writing tools. In a few moments the classroom was changed into a room of scientists. How often, after all, do we get a chance to experiment with a gas that is lighter than the air we breathe?

As soon as everyone had their materials, I too began experimenting with my helium-filled balloon. At the same time, I was making rounds to see how everyone was doing. Michelle, whose idea it was to begin this experiment, was tying a tack onto her balloon to see if it would be held up.

"What do you think it will do?" I asked. She showed me her chart with the word *tack* in one column labeled "Item" and a check under her "Yes" column. "So you think your balloon will lift it up?"

"Um hmm," she murmured as she lifted her first trial up and let it go. The weight of the tack slowly pulled the balloon to the floor. Undeterred, Michelle quickly checked the "no" column and put a circle around it (Figure E–12). "That's so I can tell which ones I got right and which ones I got wrong."

"That's a nice idea. Mind if I share that with the class?"

"Sure," she replied, already looking around for something light to test.

When I reported to the class that Michelle was recording what she was testing and whether or not she was correct in her prediction, I could see others turning their papers over to try again. To me this was a fine compliment. Many children were taking Michelle's idea and extending it, making it their own. This was not a competition to see who could test the most things or who could make the fanciest chart. When good ideas were shared, other children often tried to incorporate them. Michelle didn't seem to even notice as she continued testing one and then two rubber bands. I find it useful sometimes to share a child's strategy in the middle of an activity so that other children have the opportunity to borrow or revise it in their own way as they continue to work.

In the meantime, Corina and Tracy were working side by side sharing ideas and small objects to test the lift of their balloons. They both had columns called "Item," "Prediction," "Yes," and "No." While they were working together and sharing ideas, there were interesting differences between their charts. Tracy made her prediction first, then tested her item and placed a check in the proper "Yes" or "No" column. If her prediction was correct she put a cloud around the checkmark. If her guess was incorrect then the check got a dark circle (Figure E–13). Corina followed a similar course but indicated whether or not the balloon would

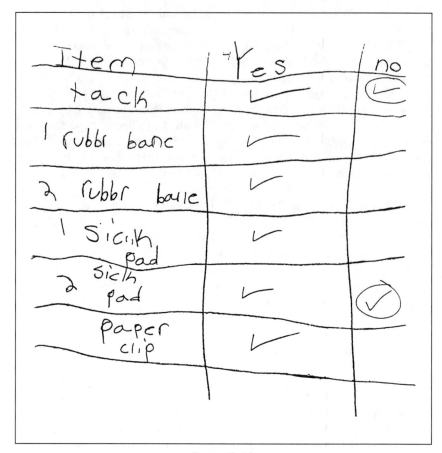

FIGURE E–12

lift the item she was testing with smiling faces. Presumably she would have used a frown face if her prediction had not been accurate (Figure E–14).

Most students had the same columns in their charts; after all, most of us had been together for one full school year in second grade and a couple of months in third. But the spirit of capitalizing on one another's successes and good ideas pervaded the class. Good ideas were copied and altered without jealousy or anger. These children were authoring in mathematics. Like professional authors, they were revising, comparing notes, running ideas by each other, and sharing their texts.

While I initially hesitated to put my plans aside—they were, after all, what I had written down in my plan book and were a logical extension of our trip to the store—I was very pleased with the outcome of our

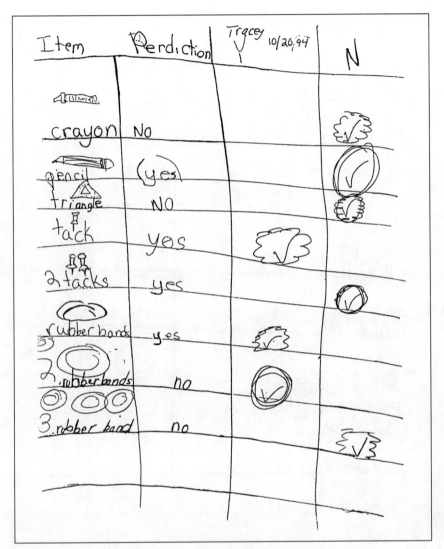

FIGURE E–13

study that morning. While testing the lift of helium balloons was nowhere in my plans for this year, the experience was an extremely valuable one at the time and it was something I referred back to when we were studying the nature of matter later on in the school year.

This experience, like so many others in my career, confirmed that it is important at times to simply put away the lesson plan book, district guidelines, and textbooks to follow your nose. Go ahead, *bird walk!* There

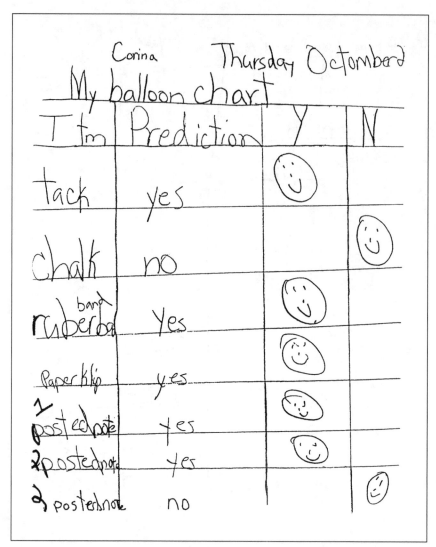

FIGURE E–14

is a depth of understanding and intuition that is beyond measure within most of us. We know our students and, when we give ourselves permission to help students seek answers to questions that are meaningful to them, we find what is possible rather than what is typical.

Lesson plans *are* important. They force us to think and plan ahead. They help us to be systematic in our instruction and they form a paper trail so that we know where we've taken our class; I went back and wrote in the helium experiment in my plan book. However, lesson plans should not limit creativity, curiosity, interest, and innovation. They should support, rather than restrict, the natural learning opportunities that arise in any classroom. These are some of my thoughts about the logistics of setting up and running my classroom. I try to highlight the functionality of mathematics, such as the use of clock faces to show our daily schedule. I establish certain mathematical rituals myself, such as using base-ten blocks or money to express the number of the day, but I also look to the children to set new rituals, such as the timing of the lunch count. I offer open-ended invitations, such as the class math journal, that invite children to record a wide range of information. I work hard to involve parents in the mathematics education of their children by encouraging them to respond to their child's homework project and by incorporating their ideas and opinions in my parent newsletter. I try to remain open to the new directions that children pose, such as testing the lifting power of helium balloons. These are some of the strategies that I have found useful as I continue to grow and change as a teacher.

And the Story Lives On

During the year-long exploration of infinity, Jonathan discovered another example of this concept that seems a fitting ending for this book (Figure E–15). He wrote: "A person has a baby. That person will tell the story and it goes on like the picture 'cause it is infinity." In his picture he drew two large circles to represent a set of parents who tell stories to their own child (small circle). This child then grows up, gets married, and tells these stories, and other stories, to his own child, who grows up, gets married, tells more stories, and so on.

This book is a collection of stories that celebrate the thinking of young children. There are stories of shoe sizes, cubit lengths, and odd and even numbers. There are stories about children who question, challenge, and debate. There are practical stories about calculating expenses and telling time; and there are imaginative stories about dividing a taco shell into an infinite number of pieces and musing about the relationship among the past, present, and future.

Although this book is coming to a close, the stories are just beginning. We've been telling stories, and we're confident that you and your children have been telling stories right along with us. We encourage you to continue to share your stories with other teachers, just as we have done with you. In this way, the cycle of storytelling continues to evolve. Infinity strikes again! Together we can all look forward to a promising future because we know that the stories of children's strengths and accomplishments help us lay claim to what really matters.

A pers has a bdy

That pers will Tell the
Sory and it gos on like
the pecher

Cos it is   infinity

Jonathan

FIGURE E–15

References

ANNO, MITSUMASA. 1983. *Anno's Mysterious Multiplying Jar.* New York: Philomel.

BARNES, DOUGLAS. 1987. *From Communication to Curriculum.* New York: Penguin.

BAUM, L. FRANK. 1993. *The Wizard of Oz.* New York: Scholastic.

———. 1985a. *The Land of Oz.* New York: Ballantine.

———. 1985b. *The Patchwork Girl of Oz.* New York: Ballantine.

BISHOP, ALAN. 1991. *Mathematics Enculturation.* Norwell, MA: Kluwer Academic Publishers.

BURKE, CAROLYN. 1991. Personal communication to authors.

DEE, RUBY. 1988. *Two Ways to Count to Ten.* New York: Holt.

EISNER, ELLIOT. 1995. "The Misunderstood Role of the Arts in Human Development." *Phi Delta Kappa* 73: 591–595.

———. 1985. *The Art of Educational Evaluation.* Philadelphia: Falmer Press.

———. 1981. "The Role of the Arts in Cognition and Curriculum." *Phi Delta Kappa* 63: 48–55.

EKKER, ERNEST. 1985. *What Is Beyond the Hill?* New York: Lippincott.

GARDNER, HOWARD. 1983. *Frames of Mind.* New York: Basic Books.

GEISEL, THEODOR. 1991. "The Lorax." *Six by Seuss.* New York: Random House.

GIGANTI, PAUL. 1992. *Each Orange Had 8 Slices.* New York: Greenwillow.

———. 1988. *How Many Snails?* New York: Greenwillow.

GOODMAN, YETTA. 1985. "Kidwatching: Observing Children in the Classroom." In *Observing the Language Learner,* ed. Angela Jaggar and M. Trika Smith–Burke. Newark, DE: International Reading Association; Urbana, IL: National Council of Teachers of English.

Hargitti, Istvan, and Magdolna Hargitti. 1994. *Symmetry: A Unifying Concept.* Bolinas, CA: Shelter Publications.

Harris, Jack. 1991. *101 Wacky Facts About Mummies.* New York: Scholastic.

Harste, Jerome. 1989. "Fostering Classroom Inquiry." Keynote Address at Whole Language Institute, Coastal Carolina. Conway, SC.

Hutchins, Pat. 1986. *The Doorbell Rang.* New York: Greenwillow.

John-Steiner, Vera. 1985. *Notebooks of the Mind.* New York: Harper & Row.

Kitchen, Bert. 1987. *Animal Numbers.* New York: Dial.

Lampert, Magdalene. 1986. "Knowing, Doing, and Teaching Multiplication." Occasional Paper No. 97. East Lansing, MI: Institute for Research on Teaching.

Lowry, Lois. 1989. *Number the Stars.* New York: Dell.

Mathews, Louise. 1995. *Gator Pie.* Littleton, MA: Sundance Publishing.

Mills, Heidi, and Jean Anne Clyde. 1990. *Portraits of Whole Language Classrooms.* Portsmouth, NH: Heinemann.

Moerbeek, Kees, and Carla Dijs. 1987. *Hot Pursuit.* Los Angeles: Universal Communications.

Myer, Rolf. 1990. *How Big is a Foot?* New York: Dial.

Napoli, Donna. 1992. *The Prince of the Pond.* New York: Dutton Children's Books.

National Council of Teachers of Mathematics. 1989. *Curriculum and Evaluation Standards for School Mathematics.* Reston, VA: NCTE.

O'Keefe, Timothy. 1995. "Kidwatching." In *Creating Classrooms for Authors and Inquirers,* Kathy Short, Jerome Harste, and Carolyn Burke. Portsmouth, NH: Heinemann.

Paulos, John. 1988. *Innumeracy.* New York: Hill & Wang.

Peet, Bill. 1986. *Zella, Zack, and Zodiac.* Boston: Houghton Mifflin.

Pinczes, Elinor A. 1995. *Remainder of One.* Boston: Houghton Mifflin.

Russo, Marisabina. 1986. *The Line Up Book.* New York: Greenwillow.

Short, Kathy, Jerome Harste, and Carolyn Burke. 1995. *Creating Classrooms for Authors and Inquirers.* Portsmouth, NH: Heinemann.

Silverstein, Shel. 1974. "Smart." *Where the Sidewalk Ends.* New York: Harper & Row.

Smith, Frank. 1988. *Joining the Literacy Club.* Portsmouth, NH: Heinemann.

STEEN, LYNN A., ed. 1990. *On the Shoulders of Giants: New Approaches to Numeracy.* Washington, DC: National Academy Press.

STEVENS, DIANE. 1990. *What Matters? A Primer for Teaching Reading.* Portsmouth, NH: Heinemann.

VIORST, JUDITH. 1978. *Alexander Who Used to Be Rich Last Sunday.* New York: Macmillan.

VYGOTSKY, LEV. [1938] 1978. *Mind in Society.* Cambridge, MA: Harvard University Press.

WATSON, DOROTHY, CAROLYN BURKE, and JEROME HARSTE. 1989. *Whole Language: Inquiring Voices.* New York: Scholastic.

WHITIN, DAVID, HEIDI MILLS, and TIMOTHY O'KEEFE. 1990. *Living and Learning Mathematics.* Portsmouth, NH: Heinemann.

WHITIN, DAVID, and SANDRA WILDE. 1995. *It's the Story That Counts: More Children's Books for Mathematical Learning K–6.* Portsmouth, NH: Heinemann.